Winning Shopping Center Designs No. 4

RETAIL REPORTING CORPORATION, NEW YORK

Retail Reporting Corporation
302 Fifth Avenue
New York, NY 10001

Distributors outside the United States and Canada
Hearst Books International
1350 Avenue of the Americas
New York, NY 10019

Library of Congress Cataloging in Publication Data:
Winning Shopping Center Designs/4

Printed in Hong Kong
ISBN 0-934590-97-4

Contents

Foreword

The submissions for the International Council of Shopping Centers 1997 International Design and Development Awards competition were truly international. There were 50 submissions, and, for the first time, over half of the submissions were for projects located outside the United States. There were 23 entries in the category of "Renovation or Expansion of an Existing Project" and 27 entries in the category of "Innovative Design and Construction of a New Project." There were submissions from Australia, Brazil, Paraguay, New Zealand, the United Kingdom, Indonesia, the United Arab Emirates, Zimbabwe, Turkey, Japan, Argentina, and Portugal.

Review of the submissions was stimulating for the members of the Awards committee, all of whom work with dedication and enthusiasm. I am grateful to the individual members of the committee for the gift of their time and the benefit of their wealth of experience. Our hope is that this book is not only enjoyable to the reader, but a source of inspiration for future projects.

Milton Cooper
Kimco Realty Corporation

Chairman
ICSC 1997 International Design and Development Awards

About the ICSC International Design and Development Awards

The ICSC International Design and Development Awards Program was established to recognize outstanding shopping center projects and to provide information on them to the entire industry so that others may benefit from the experiences of their colleagues.

The 1997 International Design and Development Awards Program was worldwide in scope. Participation in other ICSC Design Awards Programs, such as the Canadian or European Awards, did not preclude eligible projects from being considered for an International Design and Development Award.

This was the 21st year of the program. Projects which opened within the 18-month period, January 1, 1995 to June 30, 1996, were eligible for entry into this year's Awards Program.

Awards Categories

Categories for entries were:

Category A—Renovation or Expansion of an Existing Project
Entries had to relate to a project involving an entire shopping center, such as an enclosure, or a single facet of a center, such as an addition. The renovation or expansion must have been completed and the center fully opened for business within the 18-month period, January 1, 1995 to June 30, 1996. Eligible subject matter included, but was not limited to, improving the use of existing space, methods of keeping a center open during construction, new marketing and re-leasing approaches, refinancing techniques, innovative design and construction approaches, and adaptive reuse of the structure.

Category B—Innovative Design and Construction of a New Project
Entries had to relate to a specific new shopping center, completed and opened within the 18-month period, January 1, 1995 to June 30, 1996, and must have demonstrated how a specific design or construction problem was solved or how new standards in design or construction were established. New methods of environmental enhancement, space utilization design themes, energy conservation, and innovative construction techniques were among the subjects that were considered for this category. Entries included detailed information about the design and construction of the center, such as explanations of the reasons for, and the realized accomplishments of, the particular approach.

Awards Classifications

Entries submitted for either **category** were judged according to the following center **classification** system:

1. Projects under 150,000 square feet of total retail space*
2. Projects of 150,001 to 500,000 square feet of total retail space*
3. Projects over 500,001 square feet of total retail space.*

*Total retail space includes all square footage included in gross leasable areas (GLA), all department store or other anchor square footage, movie theaters, ice skating rinks, entertainment centers, and all peripheral (out-lot) space engaged in retail enterprise. It does not include office or hotel square footage.

Eligibility

1. The ICSC International Design and Development Awards Program was open only to ICSC member companies. Any ICSC member company could enter as many projects as desired in either of the two categories.
2. Entries must have had the authorization and signature of the owner or management company of the property.
3. Projects opened within the 18-month period, January 1, 1995 to June 30, 1996, were eligible.
4. Projects must have been completed and opened for business by June 30, 1996.
5. Separate phases of a project could be submitted individually, provided they were completed and opened for business by June 30, 1996.
6. Projects could only be submitted once. Projects that were entered in the past could not be resubmitted unless substantial changes were made since the last submission.
7. Members entering the ICSC Canadian or ICSC European Awards Programs had to submit separately to the International Design and Development Awards Program and entries had to adhere to its entry guidelines and requirements. Entries accepted to other ICSC awards programs did not automatically qualify for this program, nor was any entry excluded simply because it was an award winner in another program.

If you have any questions about the International Council of Shopping Centers International Design and Development Awards or would like to receive an application for the upcoming awards program, please write or call:

International Council of Shopping Centers
International Design and Development Awards
665 Fifth Avenue
New York, NY 10022-5370
Telephone: (212) 421-8181, ext. 320
FAX: (212) 486-0849

Acknowledgments

The International Council of Shopping Centers 1997 Design and Development Awards were selected by a committee of diverse shopping center professionals representing retailers, developers, and architects. The International Council of Shopping Centers is grateful to these judges for the time, effort, and expertise they contributed to the awards program.

Milton Cooper, *Chairman*
Kimco Realty Corporation
New Hyde Park, New York

Ronald A. Altoon, FAIA
Altoon + Porter Architects
Los Angeles, California

Jervis Dorton
The Rouse Company
Columbia, Maryland

Gordon T. Greeby
The Greeby Companies, Inc.
Lake Bluff, Illinois

Daryl K. Mangan
SAFECO Properties, Inc.
Seattle, Washington

Richard E. Montag
The Richard E. Jacobs Group
New York, New York

Rao K. Sunku
JC Penney Co., Inc.
Dallas, Texas

Ian F. Thomas
Thomas Consultants, Inc.
Vancouver, British Columbia

Gerald M. White
Copaken, White & Blitt
Leawood, Kansas

Innovative Design and Construction of a New Project

Innovative Design and Construction Of a New Project

Owner:
Fukuoka Jisho Co., Ltd.,
Sumitomo Life Insurance Co.,
Fukuoka Japan, Urban Design
Fukuoka, Kyushu
Japan

Architect/Designer:
The Jerde Partnership International, Inc.
Venice, California

Design Award

Canal City Hakata

Fukuoka, Kyushu Japan

Gross size of center:
2,400,000 sq. ft.

Gross leasable area excluding anchors:
273,700 sq. ft.

Total acreage of site:
8.4 acres

Type of center:
Regional center

Physical description:
Open mall

Location of trading area:
Urban

Population:
- Primary trading area
  2,700,000
- Secondary trading area
  4,000,000

Development schedule:
- Present center
  April 20, 1996

Parking spaces:
- Present number
  1,300
- 500 parking spaces to be added

Photos: Hiroyuki Kawano

Seen from the street at night, Canal City Hakata is an entertainment magnet.

福岡シティ劇場
CANAL CITY
WELCOME
TO
CANAL CITY
HAKATA
HMV

Canal City Hakata is the largest privately developed real estate project in Japan's history, incorporating two hotels and a business center. Its downtown combination of retail and entertainment, its developer says, is rooted in the creation of Horton Plaza in San Diego, California, in 1984.

Designed as a series of specialized districts with a canal as its "main street," Canal City Hakata integrates shopping, entertainment/cultural, office, and hotel uses into a focused development. The project sought to fuse the city of Fukuoka's three pedestrian districts into a larger, singular whole, yet respect the smaller-scale, traditional fabric surrounding the site. The scale (2.4 million sq. ft.) and density of the project demanded seamless collaboration of client, architect, and contractors.

The architects have long held that the future of cities and the challenge of retail design reside in a simple premise: raise the quality of the human experience in the places where people come together. This belief informed all aspects of designing Canal City Hakata.

In designing the project, the architects first created a place for people then, for commerce. The result is that commerce and the developer's economic objectives have been realized more successfully than in conventional, commerce-directed planning and design.

To do so, the developer and architect created an expanded design team, including landscape, environmental, graphic, water feature, and lighting designers. Client and architects worked closely together to define and implement the project's marketing, planning, operations, and leasing strategies.

An aerial view of Canal City Hakata shows the two hotels (at left and right), the multiplex (top), and the imaginative retail layout surrounding the canal.

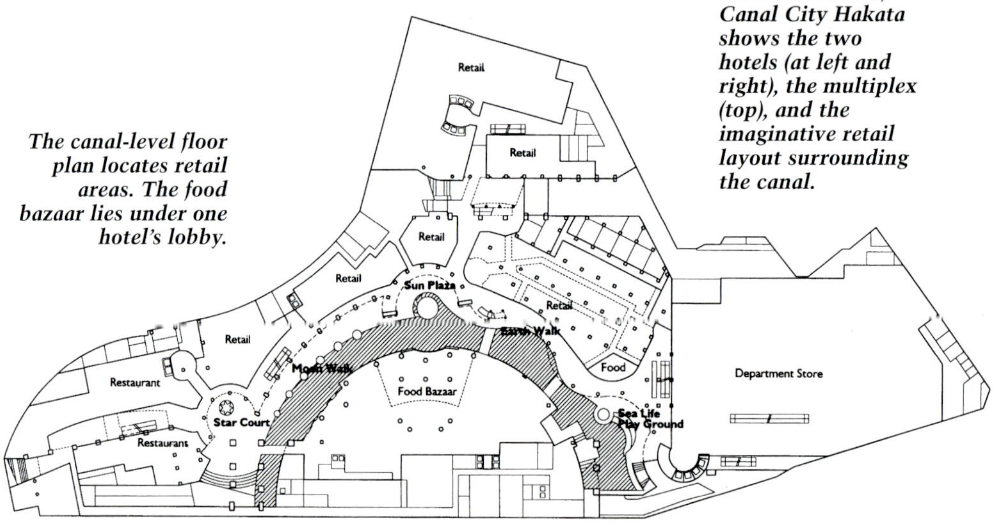

The canal-level floor plan locates retail areas. The food bazaar lies under one hotel's lobby.

For all its size, Canal City Hakata fits snugly into its surrounding community.

Plantings provide a sense of continuity between upper and lower levels.

Fountains and pools highlight Moonwalk by day, but at night the lights are the show.

A dual anchoring system was created, in which a horizontal four-anchor system was teamed with a two-level vertical system including a canal and "Broadway," an entertainment level.

The first eight months' attendance at Canal City Hakata topped 12 million visitors, but the developer says certain aspects would be redone if given the opportunity. The retail core of the project is weighted to a market segment of 16- to 30-year-olds. The project draws children and older adults, but there are not enough stores to serve this larger audience. The tenant mix is being reevaluated.

Also, the Broadway level was designed to compete with the strength of the canal level, which is the project's primary "festival" level. The Broadway level was intended to have a stronger destination pull. To realize this fully, Broadway is being reinforced with additional anchors appropriate to the original intent.

The concepts that distinguished Horton Plaza in the 1980s have evolved into Canal City Hakata, which seeks to revitalize and rehumanize communities in the 1990s. "The questions the project answers have global applications and implications. Our human environments the world over are in dire need of the infusion of new answers. Canal City Hakata is a major step forward in that process."

Storefront design ranges from the traditional to the exotic.

MAJOR TENANTS		
NAME	**TYPE**	**GLA (SQ. FT.)**
Daiei Mega Vandle	Value-based specialty store	336,117
Canal City OPA	Specialty retail and food	226,776
AMC Canal City 13	Multiplex cinema	84,573
Shiki Theatrical Company	Local city theater	67,867
Sega Joyopolis	High-tech amusement center	49,601
Mujirushi Ryohin	Department store	23,024

(Top left, top right, and left) Star Court and Sun Plaza are the venues for many live performances.

Innovative Design and Construction Of a New Project

Owner:
The Irvine Company
Newport Beach, California

Architect/Designer:
RTKL Associates, Inc.
Los Angeles, California

Design Award

Entertainment Center at Irvine Spectrum

Irvine, California United States

Gross size of center:
271,200 sq. ft.

Gross leasable area excluding anchors:
257,700 sq. ft.

Total acreage of site:
38 acres

Type of center:
Theme/festival center

Physical description:
One level

Location of trading area:
Suburban

Population:
- Primary trading area 1,575,000
- Secondary trading area 1,250,000

Development schedule:
- Present center November 22, 1995
- Future expansion July 1, 1998

Parking spaces:
Present number
- 4,304
- 1,300 parking spaces to be added

Moroccan influences are evident in the openwork design of this outdoor pavilion.

Photo: David Whitcomb 1996/RTKL

Proximity to office buildings attracts a large lunchtime crowd to the Entertainment Center at Irvine Spectrum.

Photo: Bryan Mar 1996/RTKL

A floor medallion uses the color palette of the Moroccan desert.

The site plan shows how stores "look in" on a central plaza, mirroring the style of Moroccan towns.

Original plans called for the Entertainment Center at Irvine Spectrum to be a restaurant cluster serving large office buildings nearby. Its location at the intersection of two major interstate highways, coupled with growing employment in the area and a neighboring affluent population, held promise for expanding the project with entertainment and retail.

What evolved was a gathering-place comprising a 21-screen cinema, 110,000 sq. ft of retail and entertainment uses, a 400-seat food court, and four signature restaurants. Together, they form a "main street" for the City of Irvine.

The center's Moroccan-inspired theme fits its southern California setting, yet distinguishes it from other retail and entertainment venues, whose design is largely Spanish-Mediterranean. Bolder than its Spanish counterpart and thus appropriate for an entertainment setting, Moroccan design incorporates mass, light, shadow, and color.

All graphic signage, monumentation, paving, and tile were crafted out of Moroccan textile patterns. The center looks in on itself, in the style of a Moroccan village, with buildings and spaces configured around a central plaza.

Photo: David Whitcomb 1996/RTKL

Fountains and palm trees suggest oases.

MAJOR TENANTS		
NAME	**TYPE**	**GLA (SQ. FT.)**
Edwards 21-plex Cinema	Movie theaters	158,000
Barnes & Noble	Bookstore	19,700
SegaCity	Entertainment arcade	14,700
Blockbuster Music	Music	10,000

Design images tend to suggest, rather then duplicate, natural forms.

A flexible color scheme allows distinct daytime and nighttime ambiances.

Photos: David Whitcomb 1996/RTKL

Design patterns and lighting suggest images rather than display them. Creative lighting placement and a flexible color palette allow for separate daytime and nighttime ambiances: soft and subtle shades by day become deeply saturated hues at night.

Construction faced a challenge. Due to severe rains, the construction period was cut by six weeks. To overcome the delay, personnel from all aspects of the project—landscape, graphics, lighting, architecture, and construction—were brought together for unobstructed communication on a daily basis.

The presence of the 21-screen cinema presented its own challenge —specifically, how to balance the intimate scale of the retail and entertainment area with the cinema's enormity. Spaces near the theater are wide and open, and gently narrow into more typically-sized passageways nearing the stores and restaurants. The wayfinding system, bringing people into the center, contains subdued patterns rather than blinking neon arrows.

Success exceeded expectations. The cinema has become the highest-grossing motion picture complex in the United States. The IMAX theater in the cinema building enjoys a sellout crowd on weekends. Restaurants say they are averaging 30 percent better than their own projections.

The success caused additional work. While the project originally had three times the parking required by code (5 cars to each 1,000 sq. ft), more spaces were added (bringing the ratio to 17 cars for each 1,000 sq. ft.). The developer says valet parking capacity also would have to be expanded.

Imaginative design contributed not only to the Entertainment Center at Irvine Spectrum's role as a "main street," but also to its becoming a model for themed entertainment centers.

Canopies, arches, and textures communicate the Moroccan-inspired design.

A tent motif is applied to food areas inside and out.

Photos: David Whitcomb 1996/RTKL

Innovative Design and Construction Of a New Project

Owner:
Fulcrum Capital
Sacramento, California

Architect/Designer:
Mark Dziewulski
Sacramento, California

Design Award

Rocky Ridge Town Center

Roseville, California United States

Gross size of center:
105,000 sq. ft.

Gross leasable area excluding anchors:
105,000 sq. ft.

Total acreage of site:
9.5 acres

Type of center:
Theme/festival center

Physical description:
Strip

Location of trading area:
Suburban

Population:
- Primary trading area
  80,000
- Secondary trading area
  250,000

Development schedule:
- Present center
  May 1996

Parking spaces:
- Present number
  540

Use of colored cement in the plaza defines areas for seating and customer traffic.

DeVons
BEN & JERRY'S
NEW YORK BAGELS

Rocky Ridge Town Center brought a community gathering-place to Roseville, California, a rapidly growing, affluent suburb of Sacramento which previously lacked a downtown core. The developer's intent was to give the project the sense of a small-town street, while giving local residents in search of quality dining, entertainment, and shopping plenty of reasons to skip the 20-mile drive to Sacramento.

Tenant mix has two strengths: multi-media retailers (Borders Books and Music, Blockbuster Video, Egghead Software, Learning Express, and AT&T Wireless Services) and restaurants. Previously, the developer says, no national music, software, or book retailers were available in the market. The mix emphasizes cross-shopping: some customers buy a latte at Starbucks Coffee, a bagel at Noah's, and a foreign-language newspaper at Borders.

Many eclectic structures energize the facade of Rocky Ridge Town Center.

The plaza offers a peaceful spot within the retail setting.

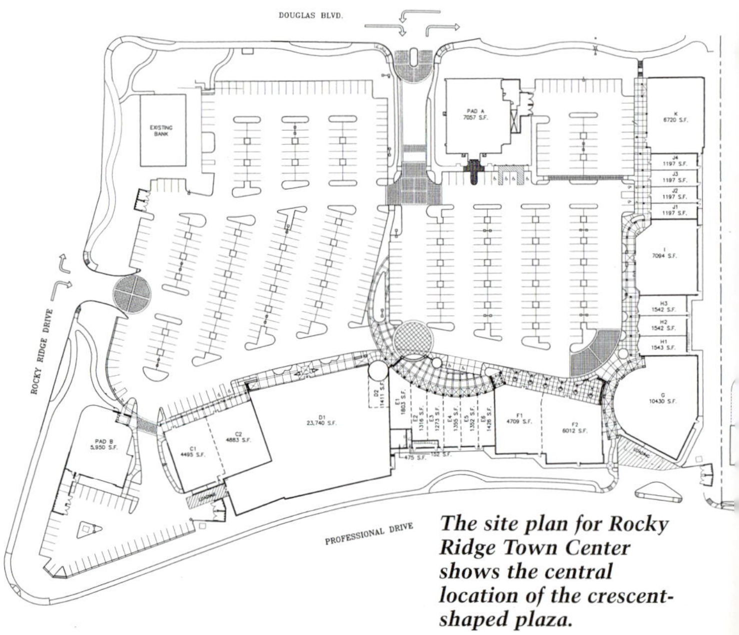

The site plan for Rocky Ridge Town Center shows the central location of the crescent-shaped plaza.

A classic L-shape for the center makes each shop visible from the main streets. The strip center is comprised of only two buildings, but stores each have an individual architectural identity, made possible by variations in the color scheme and accent materials.

Store identity is further communicated by changes in the "street line," which are in turn punctuated with arches and towers. The Blockbuster building, incorporates a 48-foot tower sheathed in internally-illuminated panels. The Starbucks Coffee building has a tower element as well.

Striking roof ornaments define turns in the street line.

Towers illuminated from within attract shoppers from nearby roads at night.

MAJOR TENANTS

NAME	TYPE	GLA (SQ. FT.)
Borders Books & Music	Books and music	29,500
Macaroni Grill	Restaurant	7,300
Egghead Software	Computer	7,100
Blockbuster Video	Video	6,800

Overall, the design blends the new with the familiar. Architectural references are deeply abstracted and often whimsical, but are interpreted through familiar materials. The "crescent area" offers design surprises such as slanted metal fins and a facade that peels away from the adjoining tower, but the repetition of storefront windows, awnings, and slate-clad columns speaks in a more traditional vernacular. The blend encourages shoppers to relax in the crescent-shaped plaza.

The plaza itself serves two purposes: a resting-place with tables and a community-focused passageway into the store area. The surface avoids a bland look by using two shades of integrally-colored cement to lend visual definition to seating areas and passageways. The developer, however, has found difficulty in matching existing coloration when segments require repair or replacement—a situation that might have been avoided using a concrete stain rather than integral color.

The developer says that Rocky Ridge demonstrates that architectural elaboration generates return through increased sales. While per-square-foot costs were higher than those of conventional design, costs were controlled by confining use of expensive materials to high-traffic, high-touch locations —for example, column bases near store entrances are clad with imported and domestic stone.

High-design concepts also attract customers. The translucent panels in the Borders and Blockbuster towers, when lit, draw drivers passing by at night.

Rocky Ridge Town Center's developer is satisfied that the project combines visual innovation with community sensitivity to the benefit of all.

Unusual architectural features provide lively arcades overhead.

Columns combine classic references with modern form.

Openings in the canopy remind shoppers of the modern design that surrounds them.

Even the rear of the center hints at individual store shapes.

Innovative Design and Construction Of a New Project

Owner:
Fortin Maure S.A.
Buenos Aires
Argentina

Architect/Designer:
Bodas • Miani • Anger Arquitectos & Asociados Elizalde
Buenos Aires
Argentina

Design Award

El Solar de la Abadía

Buenos Aires Argentina

Gross size of center:
258,336 sq. ft.

Gross leasable area excluding anchors:
105,150 sq. ft.

Total acreage of site:
1.68 acres

Type of center:
Neighborhood center

Physical description:
Two level

Location of trading area:
Urban but not downtown

Population:
- Primary trading area
  500,000
- Secondary trading area
  3,000,000

Development schedule:
- Present center
  September 21, 1995

Parking spaces:
- Present number
  220

Plantings and traditional architecture in the storefronts are in harmony with the center's surrounding neighborhood.

NDO DEL
UETE
DEL JUGUETE
EL MUNDO DEL
JUGUETE
Gimo's
NAVIDAD
En El Solar,
Navidad a toda
máquina.
El BMW Z3 de James Bond y
20.000 premios instantáneos.
Solicite sus cupones en el stand
de informes.
VISA
de la Abadía
Shopping Center
BIEN DE BELGRANO

El Solar de la Abadía is a two-level festival center facing the Abbey of Saint Benedict. Located in the residential quarter of Belgrano—the neighborhood with the greatest building growth in Buenos Aires—it enjoys excellent access to downtown and the city's northern suburbs.

Earlier, the space held a series of internal streets and old English style buildings that contained a carbonic gas plant. Market research told the developer and designer that nearby residents felt strongly about preserving the area's nineteenth-century architecture and particularly how the center would affect the abbey. The challenge was to transform four separate factory buildings into a retail mall able to lead shoppers easily from one place to another, using design concepts that would complement the adjacent abbey.

The designers did so by capitalizing on their surroundings. Natural light is used throughout the project and gives the mall its character. The use of lamp posts and street signs within the mall help create the ambiance of a small, nineteenth-century town.

Essentially, a large, new building was constructed inside an old shell. A mansard roof added one more floor to the project's commercial area. Excavation added two more floors below ground. The existing shell had to be supported while the new structure was put into place.

Leasing plans helped carry through the community concept and ensure high pedestrian flow. Leisure and food account for 40 percent of the retailers, fashion for 40 percent, and variety stores for 20 percent.

Now that the center has opened, the developer admits he would have placed the food court closer to the leisure area, the bowling alley, and cinemas. He would also have increased the leasable area and the number of retailers on the second level.

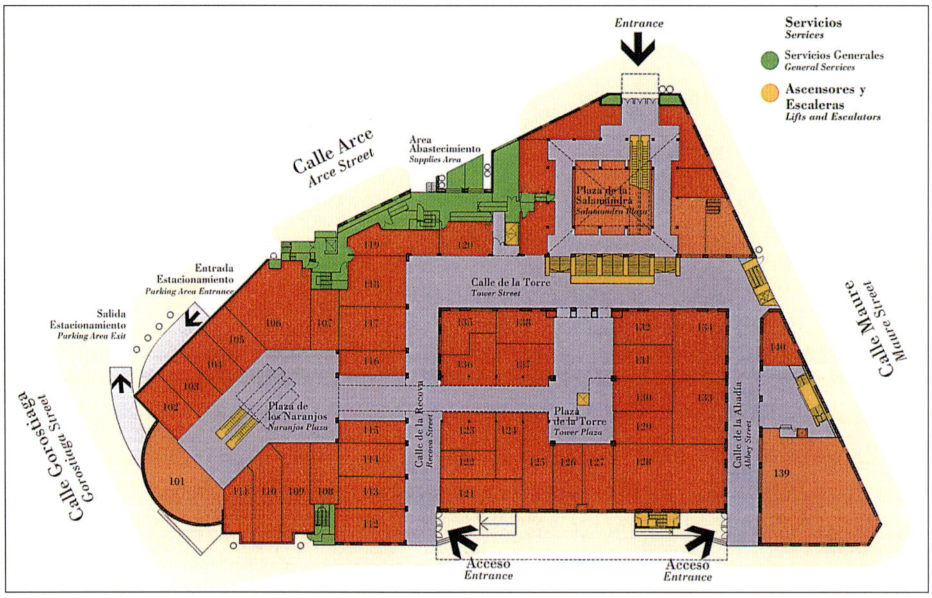

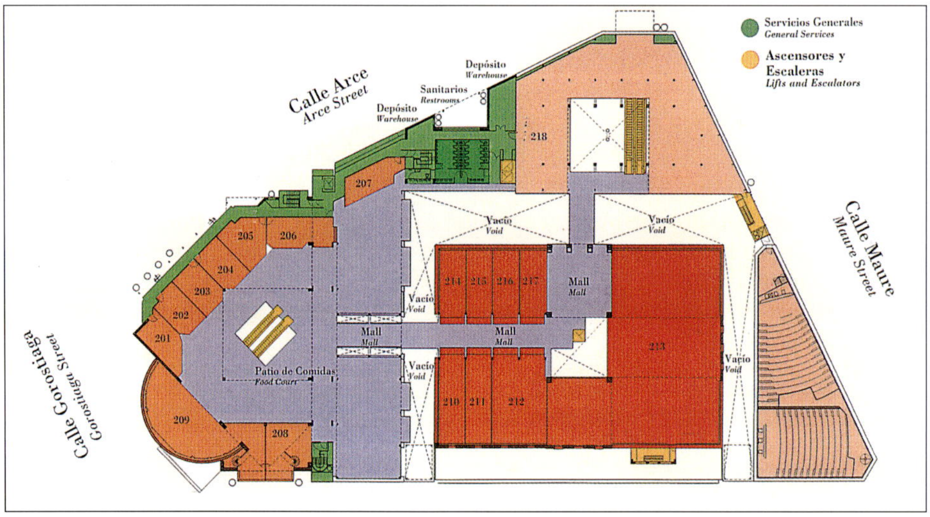

The plans for the first and second levels show the fashion-dominated lower floor and how the food court connects on the upper level.

Elements of the original nineteenth-century factory building are visible through the skylights of the center's atrium.

Even McDonald's gets the "abbey treatment."

The food court uses lively graphics and plantings to whet appetites.

Plantings and lighting fixtures lend a neighborhood feeling to storefronts.

Floor tiles and fixtures remind one of adjacent blocks.

Nonetheless, the progress and impact of the center pleased residents and retailers alike. The developer writes: "El Solar de la Abadía was the first shopping center in Argentina to open the same day the developers had planned two years before. It was actually hard to convince the retailers, since the opening of the other shopping centers had always been delayed several months .... Three months before the opening, the developers gave a reception for the future tenants inside the construction, so as to show them how advanced the building was, because they would not start working!"

From the community's perspective, El Solar de la Abadía is totally identified with the style and the culture of Belgrano. Tourist traffic in the neighborhood has picked up. The developer notes with pride: "The shopping center belongs to the place as if it had always been there."

At Christmastime, El Solar de la Abadía takes full advantage of its large, glass-enclosed atrium for displaying seasonal decor.

MAJOR TENANTS		
NAME	**TYPE**	**GLA (SQ. FT.)**
Playbowling	Bowling alley	11,086
Musimondo	Music store	6,458
Playcenter	Children's entertainment center	4,305
McDonald's	Fast food	3,230

Innovative Design and Construction Of a New Project

Owner:
Cannery Village Associates
Atlanta, Georgia

Architect:
Hiscutt and Bell, Inc.
Atlanta, Georgia

Designer:
Jeffrey A. Abrams, AIA
Peter J. Hiscutt, AIA
Atlanta, Georgia

Certificate of Merit

Abbotts Kids Village

Alpharetta, Georgia United States

Gross size of center:
41,511 sq. ft.

Total acreage of site:
7.03 acres

Type of center:
Theme/festival center

Physical description:
Strip

Location of trading area:
Suburban

Population:
- Primary trading area
  21,000
- Secondary trading area
  57,000

Development schedule:
Present center
June 1996

Parking spaces:
- Present number
  186

A flower-bedecked clock tower says that Abbotts Kids Village is indeed "time for kids."

TIME FOR KIDS

A five-acre leftover parcel and unusual market demographics led to the creation of Abbotts Kids Village in Alpharetta, Georgia, an Atlanta suburb.

After building a traditional, supermarket-anchored, neighborhood shopping center (Abbotts Village), the developer purchased adjacent land to handle stormwater retention. Five acres that remained after the pond's completion were deemed inappropriate for typical retail development due to limited road frontage. A market analysis told the developer that 24 percent of residents within a three-mile radius of the site were children under 12 years old.

The result—Abbotts Kids Village—was a shopping and activity center focused on children aged 4 to 12. At Abbotts Kids Village, the developer says, "A parent can drop off one child at swim practice, another at gymnastics practice, another at a birthday party at the plaster craft store, and then shop for children's clothing, tours, or books, or walk next door and do the grocery shopping at Abbotts Village—all within a 45-minute time frame."

All design focused on kids. The center's logo looks as though it was executed with crayons. The center's pylon sign uses a scheme of primary and secondary colors. Folk art flowers and unique clock hands are used on the clock tower.

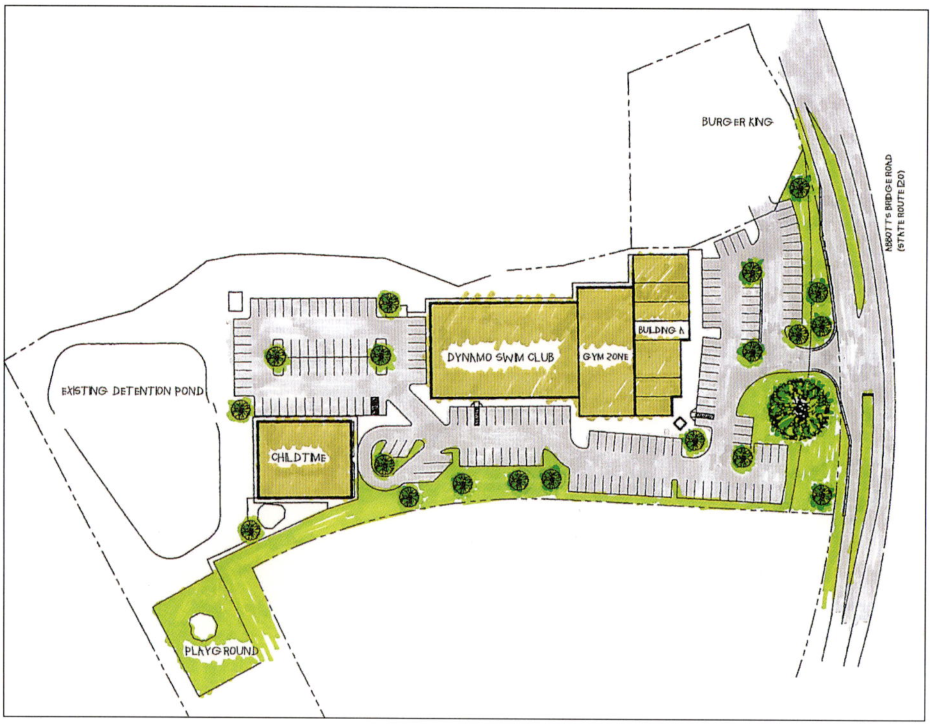

Child-focused "impulse" retail tenants face the limited road frontage, while recreation facilities are placed at the back of the site, with abundant parking.

The center's logo borrows the typeface from the adjacent neighborhood center, but otherwise looks like a schoolchild's crayon masterpiece.

The roadside pylon and store awnings burst with primary and secondary colors.

Directional signs are topped by cartoon-like birdhouses and contain the names of local schools. The locations of two anchors are marked by folk art sculpture of gymnasts and a swimmer, respectively. Tenants are asked to be flamboyant in their use of colors and arrangement of letters in their signage.

Sidewalks come in for play, as well. Hopscotch courts and train tracks decorate the pavement. The developer claims to be "probably the only landlord in America who encourages graffiti by providing sidewalk chalk to all children."

Typical approaches to retail design were reexamined for Abbotts Kids Village. For example, instead of picking light fixtures out of a catalog, the developer hired a craftsman who specializes in children's night lights. Customer amenities were studied as well, and the developer found that this center would require more amenities than most, if the center's ambiance was to be memorable to the child.

Playful storefront displays show that kids are the main focus here.

Sidewalks at Abbotts Kids Village serve many purposes beyond just getting visitors from store to store.

Graffiti artists scribble away, with the landlord's full approval.

A second Kids Village will benefit from the developer's learning experience on the Alpharetta project. The mixing of standard concrete block/bar joist-type construction with the metal building construction will be abandoned. The second Kids Village will have more common area to allow for children's performances (puppetry, dance, and music). The developer says that the new project will have a better pedestrian connection to the adjacent supermarket-anchored neighborhood center.

Over 500 kids and their "tag-along" parents visit Abbotts Kids Village each day. The gymnastics and swimming facilities already have waiting lists. One specialty merchant who relocated from a neighboring center reported a 40 percent sales growth in three months. Merchants say their customer draw is as great as 10 miles, far more than the typical 3-mile radius of traditional neighborhood centers.

Ties to the community will grow as the center matures. Plans are already underway to restore, on the center site, the second oldest house in the county. The 1835 house will be reconstructed under a 100-year-old oak at the front of the center and used as a facility for storytelling and community events. Water fountain proceeds are donated to the Georgia Council on Child Abuse. The center also supports Little League teams and has granted a wish for a terminally-ill child through the Children's Wish Foundation.

A sculpture of tumblers identifies the gymnastics facility.

The pool center's roofline shows the figure of a swimmer outracing a shark.

This charming "fuzz head" character adorns much of the center's signage.

Cartoon-like directional signage gives distances to local schools, not the center's stores.

MAJOR TENANTS		
NAME	TYPE	GLA (SQ. FT.)
Dynamo Swim Club	Pool	16,000
Gym Zone	Gymnastics	8,232
Childtime Daycare	Child care	8,107

Innovative Design and Construction Of a New Project

Owner:
City of Indianapolis, Circle Centre Development Corporation, Simon DeBartolo Group
Indianapolis, Indiana

Architect:
Centre Venture
Indianapolis, Indiana

Designer:
Ehrenkrantz & Eckstut Architects
New York, New York

Certificate of Merit

Circle Centre

Indianapolis, Indiana United States

Gross size of center:
800,000 sq. ft.

Gross leasable area excluding anchors:
368,217 sq. ft.

Total acreage of site:
N/A

Type of center:
Regional center

Physical description:
Four-level enclosed mall

Location of trading area:
Urban

Population:
- Primary trading area 1,475,736
- Secondary trading area 742,049

Development schedule:
- Present center September 8, 1995

Parking spaces:
- Present number 3,000

Circle Centre's corner entrance makes a bold statement in its downtown urban setting.

CIRCLE CENTRE
NORDSTROM
St. Elmo
STEAK HOUSE

Except for the proximity of stores on both sides, there is little in Circle Centre to disturb the idea that one is on a typical downtown shopping street.

The primary design challenge for Circle Centre was to integrate a large-scale, state-of-the-art retail mall into the historic retail center of downtown Indianapolis.

Components of the project include an 800,000 sq. ft. retail mall, an entertainment center, an eight-story parking garage, and a domed "Artsgarden." The design speaks to both preservationist and commercial interests by looking like part of downtown, keeping streets and sidewalks busy, and making every block and corner different.

Circle Centre synthesizes new construction, existing buildings, and restored historic facades. Its arcade and other public spaces are modeled on the interior shopping arcades of Europe. Major attractions include

Circle Centre's environment is a historic retail center in downtown Indianapolis.

Nordstrom entrances show how unobtrusively Circle Centre blends in with existing downtown structures.

two high-end department stores, full-service restaurants, nightclubs, a nine-screen theater, and virtual reality entertainment.

The design is intended to be both elegant and simple: an unbroken, linear arcade punctuated at several points with wider spaces to mark special functions, such as a major entrance, connection, or public gathering place. Two major nodes are courts that serve as entries to the anchor department stores. One houses the food court and is lit to emphasize daytime, the other is hued for nighttime.

The Nordstrom Court has a nighttime motif, featuring zodiac symbols (right), while the food court (below) is designed for a daytime effect.

The Artsgarden grew from the need to cross expansive thoroughfares in connecting the mall to neighboring hotels and office towers. With a bulkhead of Indiana limestone and concentric arches that soar 70 feet above its main floor, the Artsgarden links four street corners at an upper-mall level, while allowing vehicular traffic to pass below. The Artsgarden provides a year-round space for meeting friends, enjoying a concert or a fine arts exhibition, or simply having a meal.

One of the features that distinguished Circle Centre from other projects was that it was a public-private partnership beyond its financial structuring. The developer credits a high level of communication from the city, the community, the retailers, the preservationists, and others that eventually helped each constituency feel a sense of accomplishment and ownership in the finished project.

Circle Centre claims great success in many of its goals: revitalizing a city's traditional retail district, renewing downtown vitality, attracting financial investment back to the city center, preserving significant historic structures and the pedestrian character of downtown, and establishing a new public space for art and culture. This was achieved with a design concept that matches neighboring blocks and does not compromise modern retail standards.

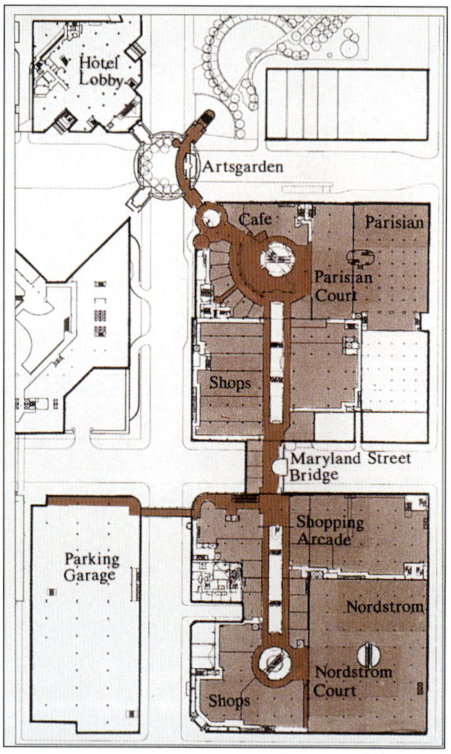

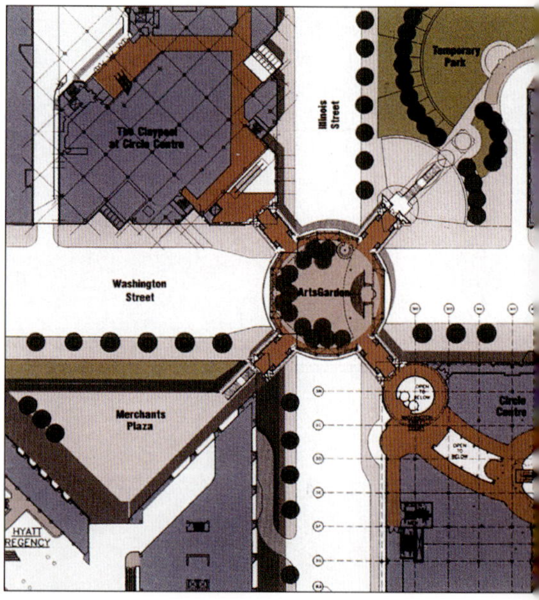

Schematics of an upper-level mall floor and the city streets show how the Artsgarden connects several city streetcorners.

The Artsgarden serves vehicular and pedestrian needs with an elegant glass dome.

The Artsgarden provides a vast public space for performances.

Storefronts are arranged in a linear fashion, providing downtown shoppers with plenty of opportunities for strolling.

MAJOR TENANTS

NAME	TYPE	GLA (SQ. FT.)
Nordstrom	Department store	206,000
Parisian	Department store	144,000
Entertainment	Entertainment	78,789

Innovative Design and Construction Of a New Project

Owner:
Majid Al Futtaim Investments, LLC
Dubai
United Arab Emirates

Architect:
Schuster Pechtold and Partners
Dubai
United Arab Emirates

Designer:
Callison Architecture, Inc.
Seattle, Washington

Certificate of Merit

Deira City Centre

Dubai United Arab Emirates

Gross size of center:
700,000 sq. ft.

Gross leasable area excluding anchors:
221,566 sq. ft.

Total acreage of site:
25 acres

Type of center:
Regional center

Physical description:
Two-level enclosed mall

Location of trading area:
Urban but not downtown

Population:
- Primary trading area
  750,000
- Secondary trading area
  1,000,000

Development schedule:
- Present center
  November 1995
- Future expansion
  Spring 1997

Parking spaces:
- Present number
  3,930

Plantings, seating, and pastel colors throughout contribute to Deira City Centre's image as a community gathering place.

Bold, illuminated graphics mark entrances.

A roof overhead blocks out the harsh sunlight, aiding climate control.

MAJOR TENANTS		
NAME	**TYPE**	**GLA (SQ. FT.)**
Continent	Hypermarket	175,677
Ikea	Home furnishings	77,097
Magic Planet	Entertainment center	59,400
Woolworth	Department store	57,908

Native tent-like structures attract shoppers at night.

Deira City Centre in Dubai, UAE, was conceived as the first shopping center to serve the needs of a middle- and upper-income market in this major travel hub and duty-free shopping zone between Europe and Asia. Its operational design and architectural decisions were made with close attention to local culture. The center is meant to be the first phase of a mixed-use project that will include a hotel, service apartments, and offices.

The climatic demands were paramount. Given the harsh environment, shaded parking proves a significant amenity, so the shopping center was elevated one level to provide parking under the building close to entrances. Two-thirds of the 3,000 spaces are shaded. Travelators provide convenient, vertical access to the mall while also facilitating shopping cart movement.

Natural light, while desirable, needed to be controlled for energy and comfort reasons. Dramatic tent structures at the courts suggest traditional Bedouin forms and combine with clerestory glazing and conventional skylights to provide a suitable and efficient amount of lighting during the day.

Leasing reflects cultural preferences as well. Shopping traditions in the Middle East emphasize groups of "souk" or "bazaar" tenants—similar types of merchants who gather to sell their wares (gold, spices, produce, etc.). Deira City Centre embraced these traditions by incorporating its own souks for merchants of gold, women's clothing, and housewares.

Operationally, the center accommodates its customers. Middle Easterners tend to shop toward the end of the day and into the evening, since a long midday break during the hottest part of the day is typical. Deira City Centre stays open from 10 a.m. to 10 p.m. (except on Friday, when shorter hours respect religious custom). To attract evening shoppers, the center uses bold, illuminated tent structures and vibrant graphics. The center also has men's and women's prayer rooms.

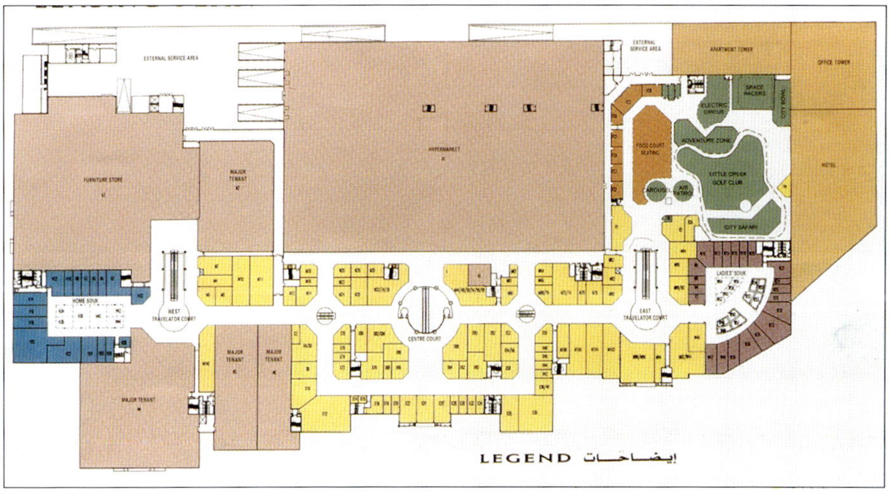

At Deira City Centre, small shops are located in front of the hypermarket. Souk-style shopping for ladies' apparel and housewares is clustered at opposite ends of the mall.

A riot of color welcomes hungry shoppers to the food court.

Extensive market research (which the developer says is rare in Dubai development) preceded design. Most of the other shopping centers in Dubai host upscale tenants, so Deira City Centre targets entire families and working-class customers. The center's value-oriented anchors—Continent Hypermarket, Woolworth, and Ikea —make their UAE debut at Deira City Centre. A wide variety of products are offered in 170 shops. A 50,000 sq. ft. amusement complex contains rides, miniature golf, and a bowling alley, plus a 500-seat international food court.

As with its counterparts everywhere, location has played an important role in the center's success. The center is five minutes from the international airport and can attract travelers from Europe, Asia, and Africa to its duty-free shopping. The mall is also centrally located for easy access to customers coming from all parts of Dubai.

To benefit from a designer's experience, the developer brought in a US-based firm, located over 8,000 miles from Dubai. Success in the construction phase depended largely on two principles. First, the architect had to understand local construction practices, among them that automated constuction practices used in the West are often achieved in the Middle East through manual labor. Second, on-site representation by the designer was very helpful.

The developer notes that the project was fully leased at opening; customer visits per day easily meet projections and sometimes triple expectations; and profitability continues to rise. A third level for Deira City Centre is scheduled to open in the spring of 1997.

Elegant design elements.

Storefronts are loaded with merchandise, showing that some retail and service concepts work worldwide.

Local customs are respected, even as travelators move Dubai shoppers into the twenty-first century at Deira City Centre.

Certificate of Merit

Eastgate

Harare
Zimbabwe

Owner:
Old Mutual Properties—Zimbabwe
Harare
Zimbabwe

Architect:
Pearce Partnership
Harare
Zimbabwe

Designer:
Development Design Group, Inc.
Baltimore, Maryland

Gross size of center:
84,335 sq. ft.

Gross leasable area excluding anchors:
55,360 sq. ft.

Total acreage of site:
2.5 acres

Type of center:
Fashion/specialty center

Physical description:
Two-level open-ended mall between nine-story office buildings

Location of trading area:
Urban central business district

Population:
- Primary trading area
  1,000,000

Development schedule:
- Present center
  April 1, 1996

Parking spaces:
- Present number
  450

An elaborate network of metal bridges and staircases connects Eastgate with neighboring multistory office buildings.

Eastgate's atrium opens directly onto the streets of Harare.

Eastgate, an urban pedestrian shopping plaza in Harare, Zimbabwe, is unique not only in its design, but also in its distinction as the first building in Africa to rely entirely on natural means for building temperature and ventilation.

With 50 stores and Zimbabwe's first food court, Eastgate is a covered, outdoor anchor for the largest mixed-use commercial building in Harare. The project also contains 290,000 sq. ft. of office space. The 476-foot, open-ended retail atrium was designed to maintain the open-air feel of traditional African markets and meeting places.

Eastgate's developer faced great challenges in wedding the desire for open-air African ambiance to a comfortable climate for shopping. Harare's high altitude, eight-month warm, dry season and four months of increased heat, humidity, and long hours of sunlight all contribute to extreme daily temperature differentials.

Working to a detailed brief from the owner, the architects first sought to minimize the building's heat gain. External walls are shielded from direct sunlight by large overhangs. The window-to-wall ratio on the

Overhangs, plantings, solar panels, and chimneys contribute to the all-natural climate control of Eastgate.

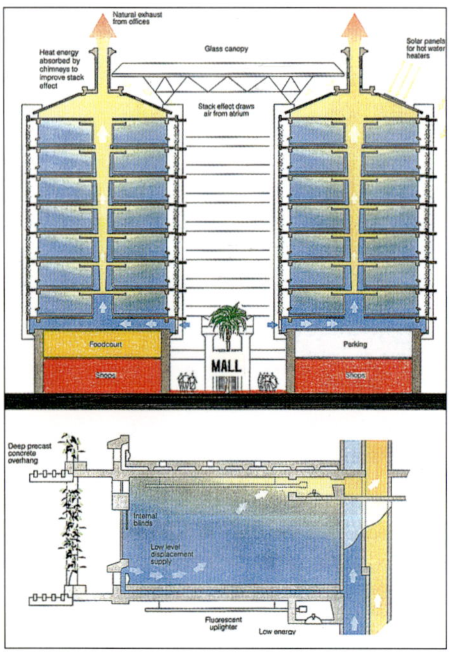

Columns and ceiling-level ornamentation unify the designs of first-floor storefronts and the upper-level food court.

sunny north face does not exceed 25 percent. Windows are sealed to avoid climatic influence. Eastgate's exterior design, which celebrates Zimbabwean cloth patterns, also serves to control temperature, since the "bristled" effect increases area through which heat is lost or retained.

Within the atrium, cool, clean, fresh air is brought in two to three times each hour through large fans, which distribute the air around under-floor concrete slabs throughout the center. The slabs help cool the air through a very low-pressure convection system. An extensive series of ducts and chimneys allow heated air to vent. Finally, the mall, atrium, and balconies are each designed with cave-like rock overhangs, which are conducive to plant growth.

None of Eastgate's tenants—retail or office users—have installed conventional electrical or mechanical air-conditioning systems. Peak electrical demand is estimated to be one-twentieth of that of conventional air conditioning. Further economics will be achieved as the building's concrete ages and cools.

The "bristled" effect of Eastgate's exterior was designed in part to achieve climate control.

Store signage successfully attracts shoppers' eyes even in a busy setting.

Beyond its unique climate control process, Eastgate also serves its community. The atrium is open and connected to the street at both ends. Indeed, it incorporates the city's street grid. Seating near mall entrances, street theater stages, and fountains all add to the interaction between Eastgate and its urban neighborhood.

Eastgate's opening provided Zimbabwe residents with previously unavailable international retailers. Given the chance to revise the existing plan, the developer says he would add a full second-floor retail level and expand the food court.

The people and materials involved in building Eastgate are virtually all Zimbabwean. The slabs and projections of Eastgate's exterior are made of locally-mined aggregates which match the colors of nearby granite kopjes (outcrops). Latticed bridge beams in the center use the same technology as the historic Victoria Falls Bridge, and elevator cars look like mineshaft cages.

Colored graphics and lighting, particularly of the main glazed-floor bridge, remove any sense of oppression from the overhangs and the office towers. Special lighting enhances the decor in the evening.

Eastgate has been well received by professionals and residents alike. Canadian and British architectural reviews and positive comments from Germany's "Green Party" have lauded the ground-breaking project for its environmental sensitivity.

The mix of local hues with escalators, metal bridges, and staircases adds to Eastgate's uniqueness.

Colorful floors and a fountain got special design treatment at Eastgate.

MAJOR TENANTS		
NAME	**TYPE**	**GLA (SQ. FT.)**
Edgar's	Family fashion store	7,298
Truworth's	Fashion store	4,553

Innovative Design and Construction Of a New Project

Owner:
Martinez Navarro y Cia. S.A.
Mar del Plata, Buenos Aires
Argentina

Architect/Designer:
Mariani-Perez Maraviglia-Zurdo Pfeifer
Mar del Plata, Buenos Aires
Argentina

Certificate of Merit

Los Gallegos Shopping

Mar del Plata Argentina

Gross size of center:
247,578 sq. ft.

Gross leasable area excluding anchors:
53,821 sq. ft.

Total acreage of site:
1.3 acres

Type of center:
Regional center

Physical description:
Three-level enclosed mall

Location of trading area:
Urban

Population:
- Primary trading area
  700,000
- Secondary trading area
  350,000

Development schedule:
- Present center
  January 1995
- Future expansion
  January 1998

Parking spaces:
- Present number
  200
- 50 parking spaces to be added

The urban feel of Mar del Plata is reflected inside Los Gallegos Shopping.

Legacy
GRIS

The food court offers variety in well-lit, compact surroundings.

Plants and flags of many nations provide visual accents to the busy retail activities.

In 1978, the Los Gallegos store burned down. In the fire, Mar del Plata (one of Argentina's most important cities) lost a key downtown retailer. The store was rebuilt in 1980 and, by 1993, the owners decided to attach a shopping center to the department store.

Los Gallegos Shopping opened its doors in January 1995. Its launch was treated with historical attention from the local press, due to its ties with the old Los Gallegos store, which had opened 85 years earlier.

The center has three shopping levels and two parking/service levels. The ground level holds the anchor store, fashion shops, and such public amenities as a cafeteria, bank, and post office. One level up, shoppers find fast food and stores specializing in sports, electronics, and toys. The top level contains cinemas and other entertainment outlets.

Levels are connected by public and service elevators, mechanical escalators, and stairs. In all, Los Gallegos Shopping contains 55 commercial shops and 10 food shops, plus 450 seats at the food court.

Cut-throughs to lower floors allow Los Gallegos Shopping to function as a unified whole.

MAJOR TENANTS

NAME	TYPE	GLA (SQ. FT.)
Los Gallegos	Department store	75,350

A bright white overhang helps identify the entertainment floor.

Several design problems presented themselves early on. Primary was the irregular shape of the property and the need to "fit" the center between several different buildings and two adjacent streets. Soft soil necessitated involvement of a German company to develop a concrete foundation.

The intersecting adjacent streets inspired a glass, shipshaped structure. The glass provides an atrium, offering natural light to all levels.

Interior spaces were carefully prepared for the hard winter of Mar del Plata, with rains, low temperatures, and high wind. Elements found throughout the city—stones, water, flags, and green plants—make the shopper feel welcome.

The project has revitalized an empty, busy corner of the community, returning a familiar gathering place to the residents. The developers say they would "have liked to build the complete original project, which included a larger entertainment area, with more cinemas." Nonetheless, over 15 million visitors toured Los Gallegos Shopping in its first two years.

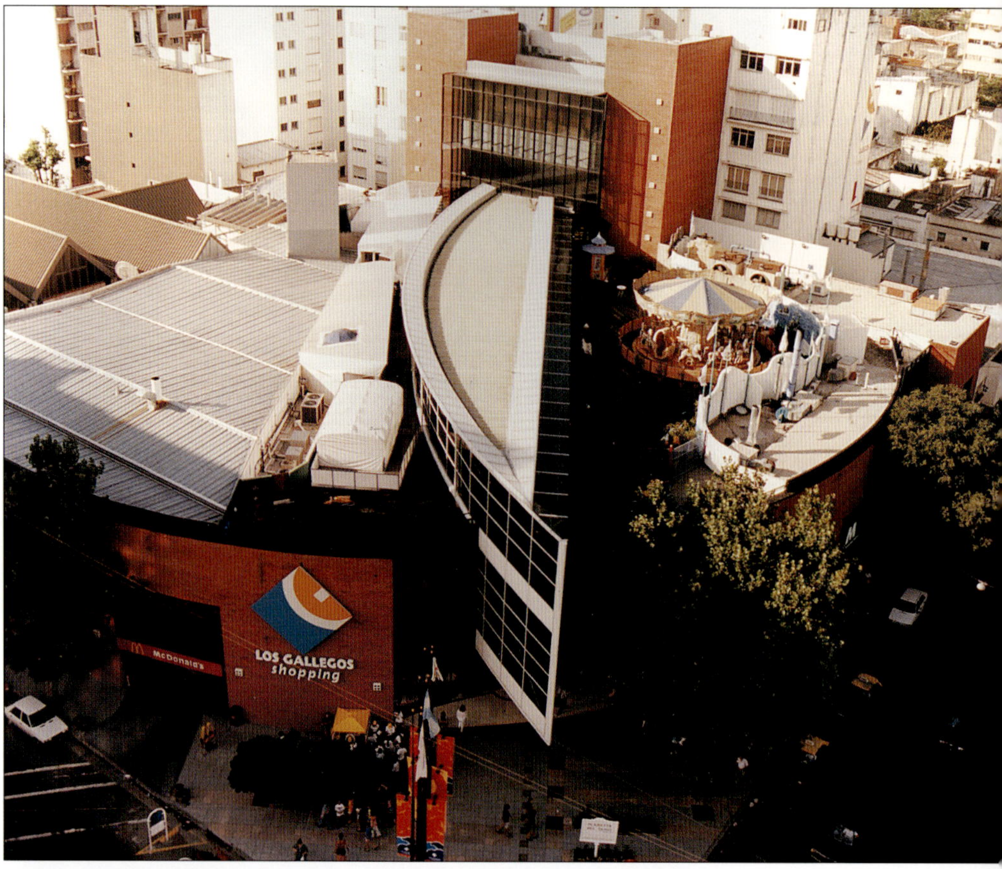

Los Gallegos Shopping has a strong street presence with its striking, shipshaped symbol.

The site plan shows how the center fits into existing buildings and adjacent streets.

Storefront design brings forth the international identity of many chains.

A thematic restaurant adds whimsy to the retail mix.

Innovative Design and Construction Of a New Project

Owner:
Ancar, Vicunha, Conshopping, Fator, Participa
Rio de Janeiro, Brazil

Architect:
Designcorp Ltd.
Toronto, Ontario, Canada
Eduardo Mondolfo Arquitectos/Tecma
Rio de Janeiro, Brazil

Designer:
Designcorp Ltd.
Toronto, Ontario, Canada

Certificate of Merit

Nova America Outlet Shopping

Rio de Janeiro Brazil

Gross size of center:
240,206 sq. ft.

Gross leasable area excluding anchors:
203,020 sq. ft.

Total acreage of site:
25.4 acres

Type of center:
Outlet center

Physical description:
Enclosed mall

Location of trading area:
Urban but not downtown

Population:
- Primary trading area
  1,005,000
- Secondary trading area
  1,746,000

Development schedule:
- Present center
  October 31, 1995
- Future Expansion
  October 1997

Parking spaces:
- Present number
  1,200
- 400 parking spaces to be added

Shoppers enjoy refreshments in Nova America's lush and airy food court.

An overhead view is a reminder of the building's history.

Pylons at streetside hint at the origins of the factory-turned-mall.

The floor plan of Nova America Outlet Shopping shows how shops wrap around two main streets, with "Playland" nestled between retail strips.

MAJOR TENANTS		
NAME	**TYPE**	**GLA (SQ. FT.)**
Playland	Amusement area	19,626
Nova America Cinemas	Cinemas	16,915

Nova America Outlet Shopping is the truest kind of factory outlet: it is built out of a turn-of-the-century textile factory. It includes over 200,000 sq. ft. of leasable area, a five-screen multiplex cinema, a food court, full-service restaurants, an open-air amusement park, and a go-cart track.

Making the transition from derelict factory to an entertaining, animated, and secure outlet mall called for innovative thinking. The existing building was used as much as possible.

Adjacent buildings not designed for retail purposes were attached. The challenge of the buildings' different heights and floor levels was met with new connecting pavilions. The variety of building design was capitalized upon by using a theme for each building that reflected some aspect of life in Rio de Janeiro: Colonial Rio, dockyards, botanical gardens, and industrial Rio.

Design attention was focused on strategic areas most evident to the customer: entrances, pylons, signage, and interior facades. Daylighting in the malls was achieved through multi-story light wells created around the existing structures.

Industrial Rio is one of the themed areas in the center.

Interior facades were a focus of design attention.

Street-like fixtures (top and right) and facades relieve the factory look.

Nova America is closely tied to its community. Customer traffic has benefited from the center's location next to the metro (the developer says it is the only center in Rio so blessed). The center's landscape maintenance provides 25 young and underprivileged residents the opportunity to learn skills that will make them more employable.

A house on the property has been converted to a nonprofit, educational, caregiving facility for children of underprivileged families, who range in age from four months to five years. This daycare center allows parents to work and the 90 children to receive care and developmental stimuli. The owner and tenants fund the daycare facility.

Almost every aspect of the project presented special challenges. The developer encourages others attempting similar undertakings to find construction management with specific expertise in renovations. Leasing was rigorous, to keep the concept of an outlet mall. It was decided to turn upper floors into office space. Expansion potential exists for a second level of retail.

Nova America Outlet Shopping was a high-risk project in an unlikely and undesirable area. Yet, its developers say it has brought energy, light, and meaning to the neighboring community.

Exterior signage (left) and landscaping (above) are elements of the factory outlet.

Interior signage reflects the color scheme of the outside pavilion entranceways.

Innovative Design and Construction
Of a New Project

Owner:
Shopping Centers Paraguay
Asunción
Paraguay

Architect/Designer:
Juan Carlos Lopez y Asociados S.A.
Buenos Aires
Argentina

Certificate of Merit

Shopping del Sol

Asunción
Paraguay

Gross size of center:
293,865 sq. ft.

Gross leasable area excluding anchors:
204,522 sq. ft.

Total acreage of site:
14.1 acres

Type of center:
Regional center

Physical description:
Two-level enclosed mall

Location of trading area:
Urban but not downtown

Population:
- Primary trading area
  150,000
- Secondary trading area
  300,000

Development schedule:
- Present center
  October 19, 1995
- Future Expansion
  January/March 1997

Parking spaces:
- Present number
  1,000

The innovative lighting design and architectural detail add dazzle to Shopping del Sol's interior.

Shopping del Sol is an enclosed two-level mall which its developer says is the first "up-to-date experience of shopping center development in Asunción, a market characterized by a remarkable delay in the incorporation of model commercialization systems."

The center is anchored, at its lower level, by a supermarket at one end and a food court/entertainment area at the other. The upper floor anchors are a department store and, opposite, a group of well-known megastores.

Throughout the design process, high priority was given to environmental aspects. Parking areas, with a capacity of 1,000 cars, have been developed based on landscaping criteria. Respect has been shown for the existing trees, which provide natural protection from the strong sun that often beats down on Paraguay.

The main entrance is appealing by day (right) or night (below left).

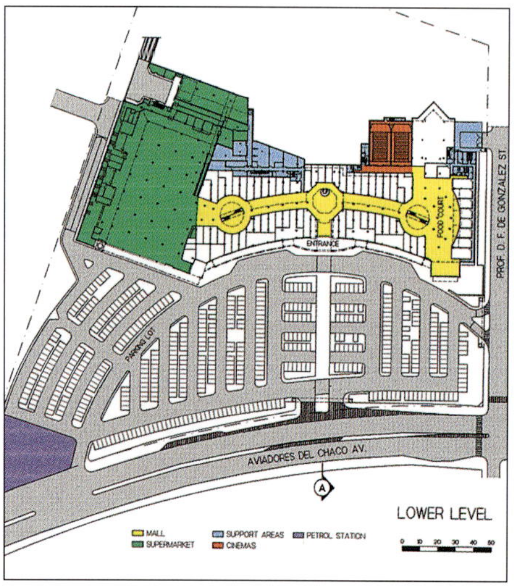

The site plan of the lower level of Shopping del Sol shows the supermarket anchor at left.

This aerial view identifies the two domed courts.

Skylights of different materials hint at the grand scale of Shopping del Sol.

MAJOR TENANTS		
NAME	**TYPE**	**GLA (SQ. FT.)**
Santa Isabel	Supermarket	64,586
Cineplex	Cinemas	12,917
Magic Park	Children's play area	7,535

The building was kept away from the property borders and surrounded by vegetation, creating a "cushion" at the perimeter. The site slopes, allowing a lower building facade facing a residential area and a double-height facade turned toward the main road.

Local materials and techniques were used, and construction benefited from a high standard of craftsmanship in the workforce. Realizing the lack of local experience with retail projects of this magnitude, the developers turned to a well-known Argentinean architect to create a shopping center similar to those found in Buenos Aires and Rio de Janeiro.

The developer says he would remake a decision to buy a small but strategic plot of land and place a gas station on it. The high impact of the center has provoked the interest of international hotel chains, which would find the lot suitable for building.

Shopping del Sol, the developer says, "is a project of the latest generation, embracing the most modern concepts with a strong identity, far from conventionalism and deeply integrated with its immediate context."

The logo of Shopping del Sol is used in both interiors and exteriors.

Shopping del Sol's garden is unexpected but welcome.

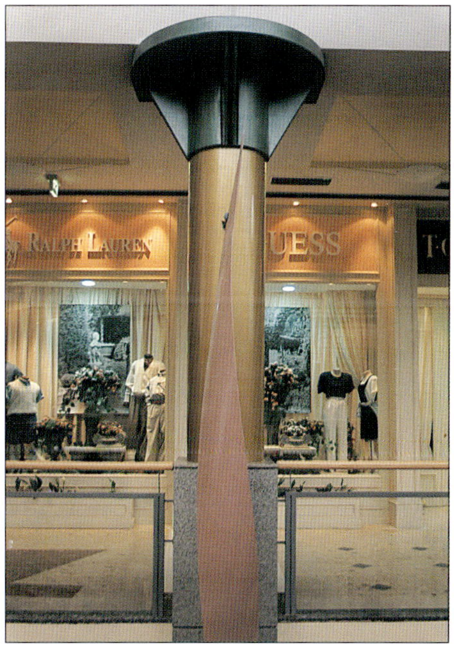

Design "extras" set the stage for high-end retailers.

Innovative Design and Construction Of a New Project

Owner:
Westminster City Center Marketplace, L.P.
Denver, Colorado

Architect:
HumphriesPoli Architects, P.C.
Denver, Colorado

Designer:
Joseph Poli
Denver, Colorado

Certificate of Merit

Westminster City Center Marketplace

Westminster, Colorado United States

Gross size of center:
340,000 sq. ft.

Gross leasable area excluding anchors:
340,000 sq. ft.

Total acreage of site:
32 acres

Type of center:
Power center

Physical description:
One-level strip

Location of trading area:
Suburban

Population:
- Primary trading area 150,719
- Secondary trading area 365,125

Development schedule:
- Present center June 1996

Parking spaces:
- Present number 1,613

Marketplace offers generous promenades, decorated with topiary.

Faced with a "not in my backyard" community reaction to plans to build a power center in Westminster's City Center district, project developers added the words "listen" and "learn" to the real estate catchphrase "location, location, location." The result was Westminster City Center Marketplace, a 340,000 sq. ft. power center on 32 acres in the heart of the City Center. It is near a regional mall in the fast-growing, northwest Denver metro area.

Initial difficulties were faced with the proposed center's very location directly across a major boulevard from the City's government hub. The site was zoned for other uses. The developer relied on quality of design of the proposed project to persuade officials and nearby residents of the appropriateness of the project. (The developer admits that, were the project to be done over again, he would "not be so resistant to public input at the front end of the project, which only resulted in extending the approval process from a typical 18 months ... to in excess of two years before we were able to commence construction.")

Painstaking efforts were taken to ensure the quality of the designed environment in its suburban setting. With an awareness of nearby city hall and by including a community park and a bike path/creek front, the center became a place not purely dependent on itself, but made better by enhancing its surroundings.

Each of the 11 building towers displays the Marketplace medallion.

MAJOR TENANTS		
NAME	**TYPE**	**GLA (SQ. FT.)**
Circuit City	Consumer electronics	58,908
HomePlace	Home furnishings	54,260
Baby Superstore	Baby and children's goods	42,900
Barnes & Noble Superstore	Books	30,554
CompUSA	Computers	26,678

The site plan for Westminster City Center Marketplace shows its proximity to residential areas and the Westminster City Center.

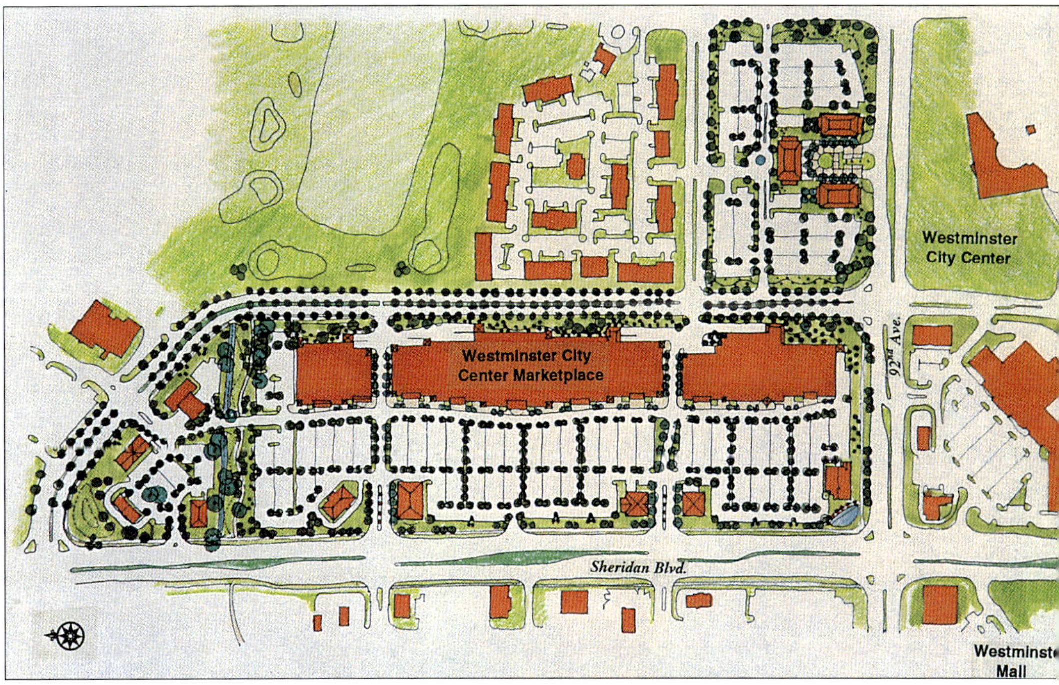

Even the Marketplace's bike path indicates classical touches, in this case, Roman-style ruins.

A wall painting of arches and columns adorns a niche outside of Starbucks Coffee.

Flying dolphins welcome visitors to the Marketplace.

Visual design at Westminster City Center Marketplace went beyond that found at traditional power centers. Marketplace was designed with complementary, coordinated building groupings, generous promenades, structured vistas, and detail in the buildings' foregrounds. A specially-commissioned bronze sculpture, "Dolphins in Flight," now serves as the landmark not just of the center, but also of the City Center district.

The concept of a city center is reflected in design as well. Pedestrian pathways from city hall, neighboring residential areas, and planned office buildings nearby are reminiscent of pre-vehicular downtowns. At key points, the pathways expand to become larger plazas with night lighting, banners, and hand-painted, Tuscan-style murals. Community events and activities such as a farmer's market, horse-drawn carriage rides, or an evening stroll for coffee or ice cream all find a place at the Marketplace.

Exterior store signage.

Handcrafted niches and tiled fountains reinforce the Tuscan theme.

Terra-cotta roofs and Tuscan-style architecture create a well-defined ambiance.

By listening to neighborhood concerns, the developer says he was able to incorporate the best of the suggestions in planning for the center, turning critics into highly-complimentary advocates. By learning from the collective experience of all members of the design team—from architects and artists to landscape planners and engineers—an uncommon marriage of the public process and profitable retailing was achieved at Westminster City Center Marketplace.

The flying dolphins at the main fountain make a dramatic sight after sundown.

Renovation or Expansion of an Existing Project

Renovation or Expansion of an Existing Project

Owner:
Urban Retail Properties Co.
Chicago, Illinois

Production Architect:
Leobl Schlossman & Hacki
Chicago, Illinois

Design Architect:
Development Design Group, Inc.
Baltimore, Maryland

Design Award

Old Orchard

Skokie, Illinois United States

Gross size of center:
1,800,000 sq. ft.

Amount of space added or renovated:
500,000 sq. ft.

Gross leasable area excluding anchors:
736,311 sq. ft.

Total acreage of site:
86 acres

Type of center:
Super-regional fashion/specialty center

Physical description:
One-level open mall

Location of trading area:
Suburban

Population:
- Primary trading area 500,000
- Secondary trading area 900,000

Development schedule:
- Original opening date Fall 1956
- Current expansion date September 6, 1995

Parking spaces:
- Present number 4,200

An outdoor garden provides a pleasant place to stroll between stores.

BLOOMINGDALE'S · SAKS FIFTH AVENUE
THE PROMENADE
FAO Schwarz
Crate&Barrel

Old Orchard is one of Chicago's oldest unenclosed regional centers. Its renovation involved adding 500,000 sq. ft of retail space, including two department stores and many upscale specialty retailers.

To return the center to its former reputation as the premier shopping destination for Chicago's North Shore communities, the center would be replanned, not to change the open-air character, but to improve customer circulation through the center and tenant access to shoppers. Previously, for example, to pass from one end of the center to the other, shoppers were forced to pass through Marshall Field's or exit into a parking lot and travel around the center. A remerchandising would be timed to coincide with the renovation.

The site itself was improved. Bountiful public space and amenities were created around a garden theme. A series of outdoor courtyards, plazas, and walkways now connected the formerly separate project elements. The garden changes with the seasons, celebrating Chicago's famous weather differentials.

Public spaces have been painstakingly planned to be people-friendly and to use the highest quality amenities. Visitors to Old Orchard now see bronzed Greek characters and ballerina statuettes, a vine-covered gazebo, white wrought-iron benches, sculptured metal, and stone and landscaped animals and fantasy creatures. Summer shoppers can cool themselves near interactive fountains, pools, and other water features.

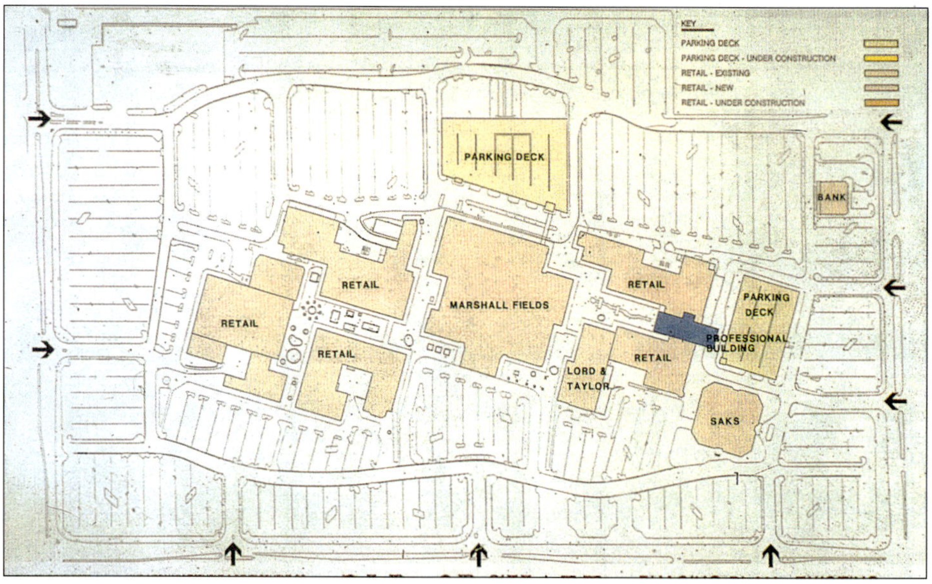

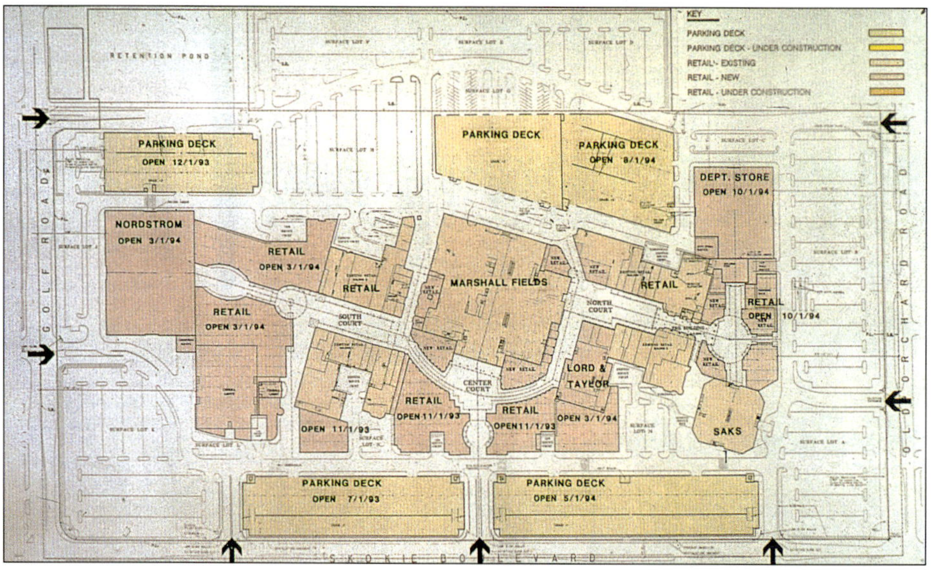

Old Orchard's former and new site plans show improved traffic flow, allowing customers to visit all anchors without passing through other buildings.

Golden flowers and matching banners welcome autumn shoppers to Old Orchard.

MAJOR TENANTS		
NAME	**TYPE**	**GLA (SQ. FT.)**
Nordstrom	Department store	200,000
Bloomingdale's	Department store	200,000
Marshall Field's	Department store	440,000
Lord & Taylor	Department store	115,000
Saks Fifth Avenue	Department store	104,000

Plantings, statuary, a gazebo, and "gaslamps" enhance the outdoor walkways at Old Orchard.

During renovation, contractors kept customers under existing outlying canopied walkways while work was confined to the central malls, and vice versa, thus ensuring overhead protection at all phases of construction. The renovation and expansion was done in 18 months, "blitzing" the entire center at once, reducing the time of customer inconvenience.

Remerchandising was extensive. Of 143 pre-renovation tenants, only 20 were asked to remain. Those staying represent high-quality retailers. Entertainment elements, including cinemas and a wider array of food options, enhanced the remerchandising.

A marketing theme of "Old Orchard Center: A Five-Star Shopping Experience" was developed, with the "five stars" not only symbolizing the five anchors, but also top quality. Print media campaigns carried out the five-star theme with a black-and-white montage motif.

The developer says that while initial discussions included enclosing the center the right decision was made by keeping it open-air. The reasoning was that Chicagoans like their climate and therefore the developer retained and enhanced the most popular aspect of Old Orchard: its outdoor nature.

Fountains and pools (above and below) add elegance to the site.

A lion and a ram lend a whimsical touch to Old Orchard.

Signage for anchors draws on the garden-inspired decor.

Renovation or Expansion of an Existing Project

Owner:
King of Prussia Associates
King of Prussia, Pennsylvania

Architect:
Thompson, Ventulett, Stainback & Associates, Inc.
Atlanta, Georgia

Designer:
J. Thomas Porter, W. Mark Carter, Donna Childs
Atlanta, Georgia

Design Award

The Plaza at King of Prussia

King of Prussia, Pennsylvania United States

Gross size of center:
1,844,543 sq. ft.

Amount of space added or renovated:
781, 475 sq. ft.

Gross leasable area excluding anchors:
301,475 sq. ft.

Total acreage of site:
93 acres

Type of center:
Super-regional center

Physical description:
Enclosed two-level mall

Location of trading area:
Suburban

Population:
- Primary trading area 1,493,342
- Secondary trading area 2,528,904

Development schedule:
- Original opening date September 1959
- Current expansion date November 1995

Parking spaces:
- Present number 13,352

Photos: Brian Gassel/TVS & Assoc.

Flower motifs enhance the Plaza's new entrance design.

The Plaza

The Court and The Plaza at King of Prussia in the Philadelphia suburbs traditionally attracted an affluent, high-fashion customer. The Plaza had focused on a popular-price-point customer base. This renovation of The Plaza comprises phases five and six, replacing and expanding the center's oldest portion.

The total redevelopment, spread over six years, was undertaken to keep the King of Prussia shopping complex competitive with existing and planned shopping centers in the Greater Philadelphia area. Over the years, the tenant roster included an eclectic mix of old family businesses and local and national chains.

By the early 1990s, Nordstrom and Neiman Marcus sought locations in the Philadelphia market. A 1991 remerchandising of The Court revealed a pent-up demand from large stores that wanted to be in The Court, but for which there was no room. The developer reasoned that if The Plaza would be upgraded to match or exceed The Court's appearance, upscale tenants would be attracted to it. Redevelopment was preferable to having these stores anchor a new high-end mall.

The Plaza was remerchandized with upscale tenants not often found in malls: Tiffany, Hermés, Louis Vuitton, Armani, Olily, Catamini, and others.

The "Welcome" sign at the new parking deck.

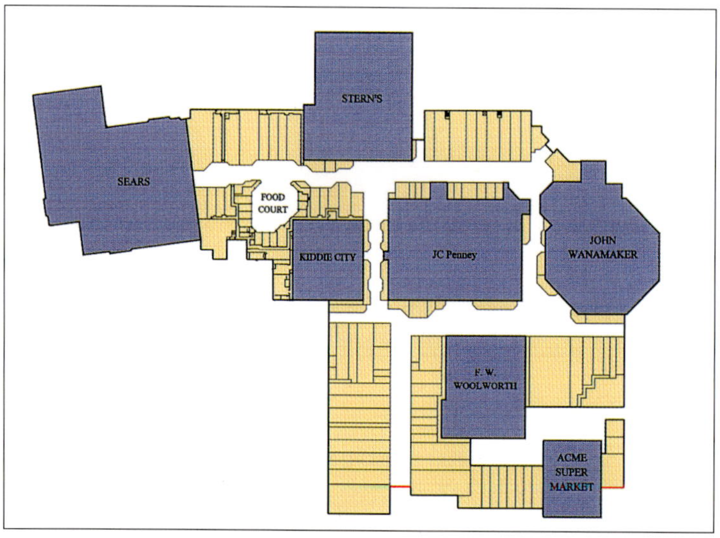

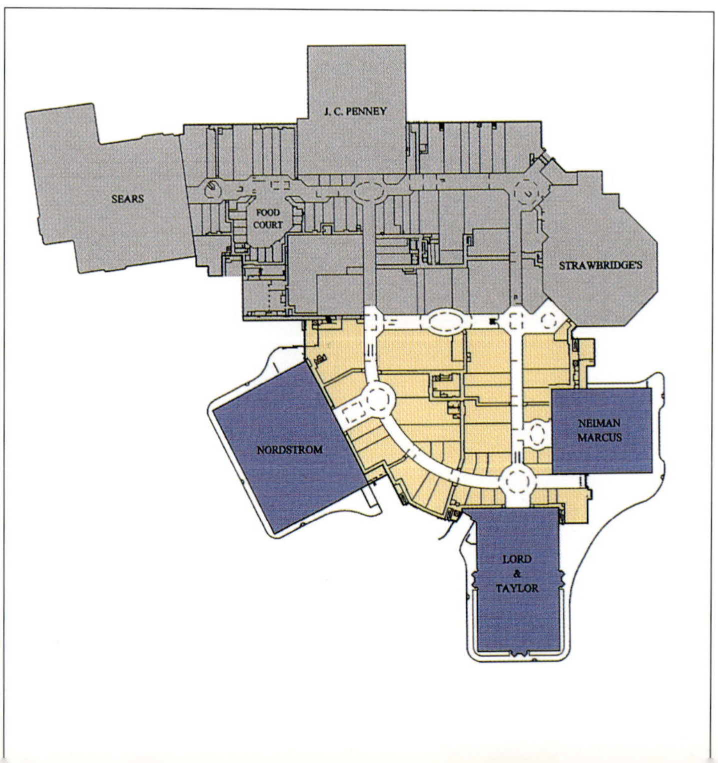

The Plaza at King of Prussia's floor plans before and after expansion show the placement of new upscale anchors.

Domed patterned skylights and large marble medallions give character to each department store court.

MAJOR TENANTS		
NAME	**TYPE**	**GLA (SQ. FT.)**
Nordstrom	Department store	225,000
Sears	Department store	222,412
Strawbridge's	Department store	193,500
JC Penney	Department store	171,558
Neiman Marcus	Department store	135,000
Lord & Taylor	Department store	120,000

A distinctive concept is used at the Cafe Court, incorporating ornamental metalwork, colonial design for an elevator tower, and a Tiffany-style ceiling.

A fountain is the focal element in the garden plaza.

The original open-air mall had retained a presence until now in The Plaza's undulating walking surfaces, old-fashioned proportions, and outdated systems of tenant buildings. The old single-level mall became a two-level format. A patterned marble floor replaced the tired quarry tile. New skylighting added colored light above the mall and department store courts. Upholstered furnishings and lush topiary created an elegant "streetscape."

The entire parking field was reconfigured, as were the on- and off-side roadways. Two multi-level parking decks added 2,400 spaces.

Marketing plans focused on repositioning The Plaza and The Court as one entity, rather than the separate markets they sought in years past. The upmarket customer was targeted through the retailing trends of the 1990s: larger-than-average stores and lifestyle merchandise, including stores for children, bath-and-body, leisure, fitness, the outdoors, and entertainment.

The decisions made for The Plaza respond to a new challenge: the aging of the first generation of shopping centers past their depreciation period. Owners of older centers must find ways to invigorate their centers or risk losing anchors to the most attractive and competitive centers around. The remerchandising, redesign, expansion, and remarketing of The Plaza at King of Prussia prove that it can be done.

Detailing highlights the perimeter of an arcade.

Renovation or Expansion of an Existing Project

Owner:
Hammerson UK Properties PLC,
The Standard Life Assurance Co.
London, United Kingdom

Architect/Designer:
Building Design Partnership
London, United Kingdom

Certificate of Merit

Brent Cross Shopping Centre

London
United Kingdom

Gross size of center:
844,000 sq. ft.

Amount of space added or renovated:
54,000 sq. ft.

Gross leasable area excluding anchors:
376,000 sq. ft.

Total acreage of site:
67 acres

Type of center:
Regional center

Physical description:
Two-level enclosed mall

Location of trading area:
Urban but not downtown

Population:
- Primary trading area
  251,400
- Secondary trading area
  1,888,400

Development schedule:
- Original opening date
  March 2, 1976
- Current expansion date
  October 20, 1995
- Future expansion
  December 2000
  300,000 sq. ft. GLA to be added

Parking spaces:
- Present number
  6,150
- 2,600 parking spaces to be added

Views of the center court at Brent Cross demonstrate modern ways of using daylight.

birdhouse

Brent Cross Shopping Centre in northwest London was the United Kingdom's first US-style two-level enclosed mall at its opening in 1976. Although operating successfully since that time, Brent Cross's premier position was under challenge from a new generation of shopping centers.

To revitalize the center for the 21st century, the owners conducted an extensive rehabilitation and small expansion, paving the way for a major expansion in the year 2000. Renovation included reroofing and refurbishing the mall and replacing the security system. New GLA totaled 54,000 sq. ft. Parking was added for 4,000 more cars.

Merchandising and operational issues needed attention as well. The center had a large proportion of its square footage devoted to anchor stores and little to food service. Strong demand existed for high-quality fashion and gift stores and international retailers. Only a single pair of escalators offered circulation between levels. The mall was artificially lit. Identity and signage were dated, as were amenity facilities and environmental and fire safety services.

An entrance to Brent Cross Shopping Centre shows the new external identity graphics.

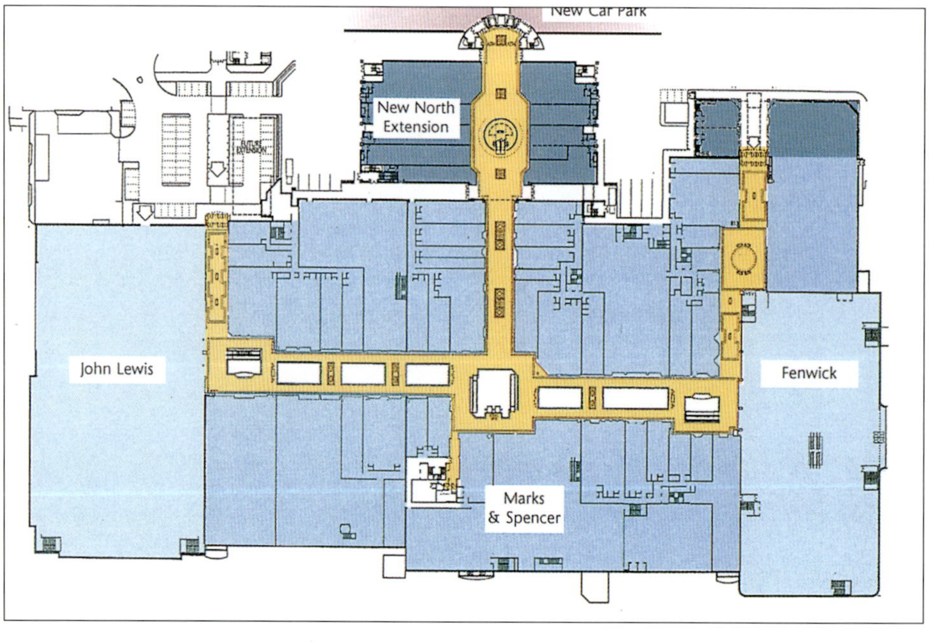

The floor plan identifies anchor locations.

Plantings adorn lower and upper levels of the new west mall.

Bright and light are key words in this view of the east mall.

Photo: The Studio, London

MAJOR TENANTS		
NAME	**TYPE**	**GLA (SQ. FT.)**
John Lewis	Department store	211,000
Fenwick	Department store	158,000
Marks & Spencer	Variety store	88,000

Through the renovation and expansion, each of these issues was addressed. In all, 13 new retail units were created in the extended mall. Five restaurants opened in a new food court. High-quality fashion retailers were attracted by the expansion and renovation plans. Eight new escalators and two scenic elevators were introduced. Daylight has been brought into the mall through glazed domes and skylights. A new identity, signage, and coordinated furniture scheme was created. Amenity facilities and the main fire and security systems were all upgraded.

Brent Cross management required that normal trading be maintained throughout the renovation and expansion period. Work in the malls was done at night, using high-level, fixed safety decks and movable platforms in conjunction with temporary roofs. Low-level work was done behind secure decorated hoardings, moved frequently to minimize obstructions in the mall.

Both tinted and clear glass are used in the north mall ceiling.

From the lower level in the north mall, there is an unobstructed view of stores above.

Land earmarked for future expansion was used for temporary parking during the renovation, allowing the demolition of existing sub-standard decked parking and construction of new, multi-level parking.

New customer services and facilities kept pace with the new look. A fully-staffed information desk, cash dispensers, and more public restrooms were installed, as were new facilities for the disabled.

A full-scale reopening marketing plan on the theme "The difference is sensational" used television, radio, poster, and press advertising. Marketing, leasing, and design strategies worked together to increase customer traffic at the expanded and refurbished Brent Cross Shopping Centre.

An extensive marketing plan, including TV spots and billboards, announced the new Brent Cross Shopping Centre.

New multi-level parking lots bring shoppers closer to their destinations.

Renovation or Expansion of an Existing Project

Owner:
Urban Retail Properties Co.
Chicago, Illinois

Architect/Designer:
Cope Linder Associates
Philadelphia, Pennsylvania

Certificate of Merit

Concord Mall

Wilmington, Delaware
United States

Gross size of center:
862,424 sq. ft.

Amount of space added or renovated:
55,052 sq. ft.

Gross leasable area excluding anchors:
363,186 sq. ft.

Total acreage of site:
60 acres

Type of center:
Regional center

Physical description:
One-level enclosed mall

Location of trading area:
Suburban

Population:
- Primary trading area
  113,977
- Secondary trading area
  176,489

Development schedule:
- Original opening date
  Fall 1968
- Current expansion date
  Spring 1995

Parking spaces:
- Present number
  4,450

Concord Mall's logo, a flock of Canada geese, "flies" above the Boscov's court.

Photo: Tom Bernard

Boscov's
HAMILTON
SALE

Photo: Tom Bernard

Concord's logo is proudly displayed on its pylon, while a mall entrance grandly welcomes visitors.

Photo: Barry Halkin

The renovation of Concord Mall in suburban Wilmington, Delaware, was done with an eye to the future.

Concord Mall's owner chose to revitalize the center after market analysis showed that the trade area had grown in size and spending capacity. New centers in the Concord Mall area would threaten its viability. No improvements had been made at the center since its opening in 1968. One anchor space was vacant. Low ceilings, few skylights and a long, sloping public corridor with concrete and brick flooring attributed to its dated look.

The owner moved to secure both short-term and long-term market dominance by developing a renovation concept that would allow future expansion on the tight site by building in capacity for an overbuild—a second level of mall shops. Short-term renovation would be completed within one year while development was being approved for the overbuild, new structured parking, and site alterations.

The renovated center provides for the overbuild in several ways. Foundations for future columns are positioned within the existing common area, avoiding future disruption to current and new tenants. New skylights are located at future openings to the second level. New kiosk "nodes" take the future space of upper-level crosswalks.

MAJOR TENANTS

NAME	TYPE	GLA (SQ. FT.)
Boscov's	Department store	175,065
Sears	Department store	174,172
Strawbridge's	Department store	150,000

Arches frame kiosk "nodes" between skylights.

Photo: Tom Bernard

A storefront before (above) and after (right) shows higher design standards.

A vacant one-story anchor space was replaced by a two-level Sears store, which is designed to align with the incoming upper mall level. An existing three-story office building extending over the mall concourse was converted to retail as a new Strawbridge's home furnishings store.

Visually, the designer sought to reflect the rural "estate" character of the Brandywine Valley region in mall entrances, graphics, and interior finishes. Design amenities include built-in planters, torchieres, ornamental column covers, rich landscaping, and stepped fountains. Planter walls, fixtures, and the choice of landscape materials were carefully planned to preserve views to the storefronts—Adonidia palms were selected for their slender trunks at eye level and graceful fronds overhead.

What had been a low, dark mall space was transformed into a series of skylit "rooms," defined by coffered ceilings and uplight coves. Arches frame the kiosk nodes between skylights and conceal the transitions in ceiling heights (made necessary by the original sloping mall). As the skylights darken at dusk, a special tier of deep blue lights switch on, giving the mall a night-sky effect.

The mall stayed fully operational during construction. Demolition and other noisy work was performed at night and cleaned up daily.

A customer services counter was added for additional sales, gift wrap, information, and car rental. Tenant releasing focused on upgrading existing storefront design and increasing the quantity and mix of national stores. Size constraints prevented building a food court, so food tenants are grouped around several courts.

Concord Mall shows that developers looking to enhance or maintain market share of current centers can benefit from early and long-range planning to secure maximum site potential, discouraging new competition.

Fountains and skylights became the focus for department store courts.

Design amenities include torchieres (left) and built-in planters (above).

Photo: Tom Bernard

Spacious and well-lit promenades lead shoppers from one store to the next.

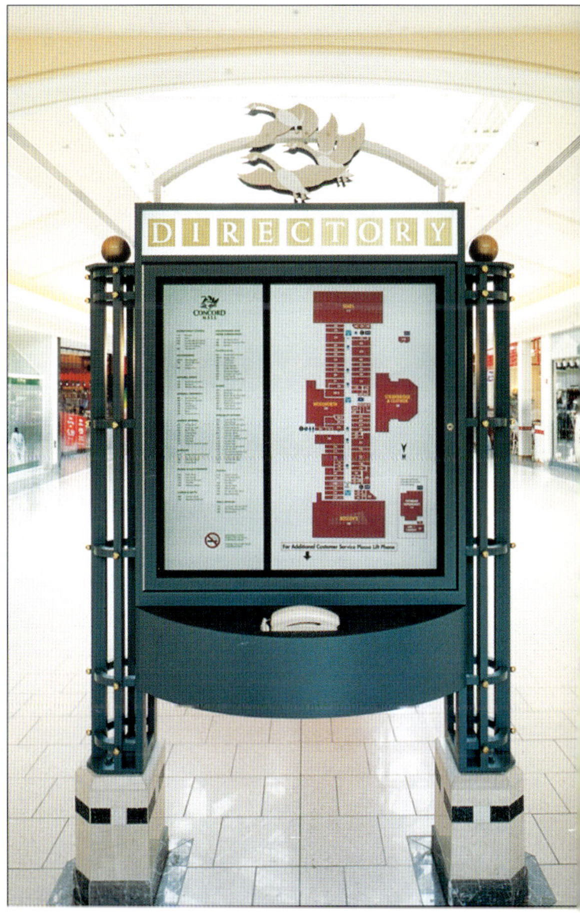

Photos: Barry Halkin

Center Court at Concord Mall gets a blue hue at night.

Concord Mall's logo tops off a new center directory.

Renovation or Expansion of an Existing Project

Owner:
Highpoint Shopping Centres Pty. Ltd.
Melbourne, Victoria
Australia

Architect/Designer:
The Buchan Group
Melbourne, Victoria
Australia

Certificate of Merit

Highpoint Shopping Centre

Melbourne, Victoria Australia

Gross size of center:
1,134,747 sq. ft.

Amount of space added or renovated:
51,480 sq. ft.

Gross leasable area excluding anchors:
483,682 sq. ft.

Total acreage of site:
67.95 acres

Type of center:
Super-regional center

Physical description:
Four level

Location of trading area:
Suburban

Population:
- Primary trading area
  64,000
- Secondary trading area
  285,000

Development schedule:
- Original opening date
  September 2, 1975
- Current expansion date
  August 15, 1995

Parking spaces:
- Present number
  5,178
- 800 parking spaces to be added

Skylights and columns bring an airy and elegant mood to Highpoint's common areas.

SaRAY
Leather
EVENTS
CAZ MAN

Glass domes brighten the Australian sky at Highpoint Shopping Centre after renovation.

Highpoint's "before" photo shows the need for a new look.

The food court benefits from the glass-and-light look.

Highpoint Shopping Centre serves the western region of Melbourne, Australia, and is nestled in its multi-cultural suburbs. Since its opening in 1975, several major extensions and development programs have seen the complex evolve into a retail and entertainment mecca. Its northern extension, which opened in 1995, brought 86 new specialty stores on two levels.

Quantitative and psychographic market research showed that within Highpoint's trade areas there were over 100,000 people who either did not shop often or did not shop at Highpoint at all. A leasing strategy was developed to attract a retailing mix to address this growth potential. The research also showed that customers wanted more shops, more amenities, and a better shopping environment.

To attract new retailers, a video called "Building on Success" and a companion colored brochure highlighted existing retail and entertainment components of the center, which include an 18-hole miniature golf course and 10 cinemas. New shops included the first Disney Store in Australia.

Interior views of Highpoint Shopping Centre show how natural light and glass ceilings lend elegance to a shopper's trip.

Additional amenities were added with deck parking to minimize the walk to Highpoint and the creation of a "Highpoint Loyalty" card for frequent shoppers, offering discounts. An atrium food court was added, containing a commissioned sculpture, "The Family," comprised of three brightly-colored, tiled figures representing a father, mother, and child.

Design took many forms. Palm trees and an abundance of natural light provide a new ambiance for the center. Illuminated glass domes make Highpoint's presence known at night. Elegant balustrades and lighting fixtures add to the shopping environment. Each tenant has a high-quality fitout to enhance the interior design and decor of the mall space.

The northern extension was built over a 15-month period with minimal disruption to the existing center, which was able to continue doing business at all times. Deck parking was intentionally built first to enable customers to park close to the center while construction continued. Customer service officers were posted in the lots to direct vehicular and pedestrian traffic. A temporary corridor allowed shoppers to access the center.

Management was able to communicate to customers and retailers through signage on the walls of the temporary corridor, newsletters, and displays throughout the center. A small number of retailers had to be temporarily relocated.

The developer had several thoughts in hindsight, including adding a Warner Bros. store, reducing the fashion component in light of impending downward trends in sales, and the introduction of another department store. The developer would also suggest that extensions be done 20 to 30 shops at a time, to lessen the impact of expansion on existing tenants.

Increases in customer traffic and sales for the months immediately following the opening of the northern extension, however, make clear that many of those non-shoppers identified in the early market research would soon find their way to Highpoint Shopping Centre.

Storefronts got fitouts and other design enhancements to match that of the mall area.

MAJOR TENANTS		
NAME	**TYPE**	**GLA (SQ. FT.)**
Myer	Department store	216,009
Big W	Discount department store	87,860
Target	Discount department store	89,352
Hoyts	Theaters	70,278

Design, too, is in the details—whether in a roof dome, balustrade, lighting fixture, or seating.

Renovation or Expansion of an Existing Project

Owner:
Corporate Property Investors
New York, New York

Architect/Designer:
RTKL Associates, Inc.
Dallas, Texas

Certificate of Merit

Lenox Square

Atlanta, Georgia
United States

Gross size of center:
1,500,000 sq. ft.

Amount of space added or renovated:
170,000 sq. ft.

Gross leasable area excluding anchors:
649,000 sq. ft.

Total acreage of site:
63 acres

Type of center:
Super-regional center

Physical description:
Two-level enclosed mixed-use center

Location of trading area:
Urban but not downtown

Population:
- Primary trading area
  800,000
- Secondary trading area
  1,600,000

Development schedule:
- Original opening date
  August 4, 1959
- Current expansion date
  November 8, 1995

Parking spaces:
- Present number
  7,000

A mural of lush foliage echoes the "real life" plantings in one of Lenox Square's main stairways.

Two entrances to the enhanced Lenox Square visually communicate elegant retailing.

An obelisk is featured in one of the center's "town squares."

Lenox Square, a super-regional mall in Atlanta's exclusive Buckhead section, underwent a thorough renovation and added 170,000 sq. ft. of leasable area well in advance of the opening of the 1996 Olympic Games there.

The expansion was undertaken to accommodate increased demands from retailers, who wanted space in the booming Atlanta market. Key Lenox Square tenants also wanted to expand.

The physical plant itself needed an upgrade. Design of a large portion of the property had not been updated in almost 20 years. Earlier expansions had resulted in a variety of design treatments. Unlike most regional malls, Lenox Square had stores facing both the exterior and interior of the mall, as well as two in-line department store anchors.

Lenox Square's design team developed a concept to evoke the mall's open-air origins and reflect the mall's position as the "town center" of the Buckhead neighborhood. Rather than addressing Lenox Square as a single structure, the designers saw it as a collection of buildings and shopping districts in an environment defined by both open and enclosed shopping streets.

The center was given two distinct types of spaces. Sunlit "town squares" in front of the department stores are meant to capture an outdoors feeling and have walls clad in limestone and plaster with ceilings of sloping glass skylights. Elegant "galleries" outside the specialty stores link the squares. The galleries convey an indoors ambiance. They are finished in Georgia marble, stainless steel, and Honduras mahogany and are identified by barrel-vaulted ceilings.

MAJOR TENANTS

NAME	TYPE	GLA (SQ. FT.)
Rich's	Department store	382,000
Macy's	Department store	274,000
Neiman Marcus	Department store	114,000

Neiman Marcus's "town square" has modern sculpture.

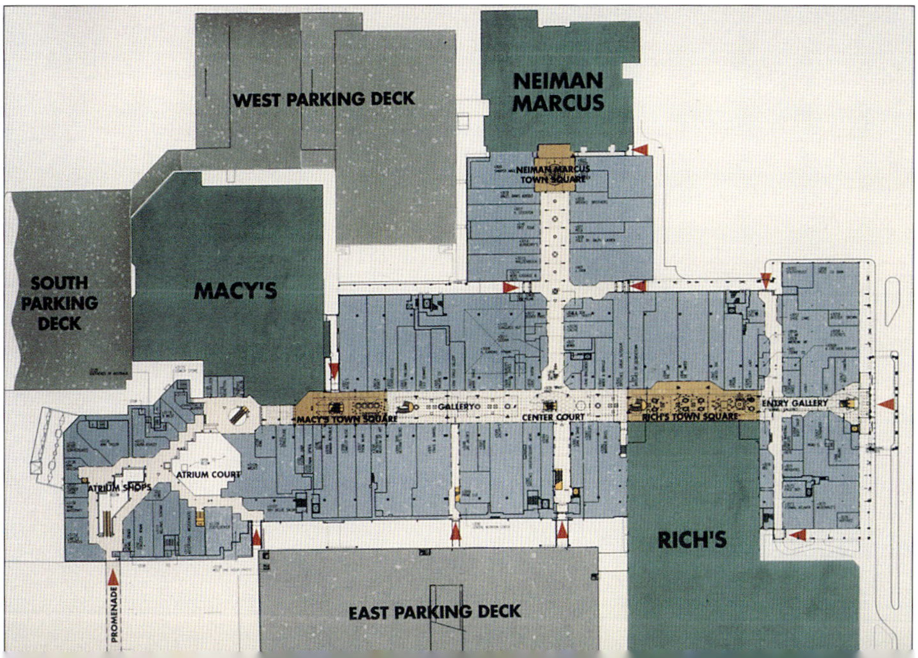

The floorplan shows how anchor stores have "town squares," which are linked by galleries.

Other improvements included a new entrance on world-famous Peachtree Road, new floors, and new graphic elements. The area of exterior-facing tenants received new finishes and became the "Plaza Shops." The food court was reconceived as the Market Court and benefited from natural light from a new two-level atrium. Parking was added.

Leasing strategies brought in stores unique to Atlanta: Pottery Barn, Crane & Co., and the Store of Knowledge. The new upper level brought in 50 upscale retailers; more than half the space on the upper level is devoted to the only stores of their chains in the Atlanta market.

Lenox Square stayed open throughout the renovation and expansion. To ensure shopper safety, most construction was done at night. Construction was scheduled to minimize heavy activity during the holiday season. Extensive scaffolding and temporary barriers shielded customers. The center was cleaned and construction debris removed every day before the mall opened.

Marketing played a key role in the project. Before the renovation, intercept surveys asked shoppers about the physical plant and many customers' suggestions were incorporated into the new design. Throughout the work, retailers and shoppers received ongoing communications through meetings, signage, and displays. Local media representatives toured the project.

Yet somehow, at the height of construction activity, Lenox Square celebrated its 35th anniversary, with major in-mall events and an extensive promotional and advertising campaign. The weekend-long celebration amid the construction garnered media coverage and increased shopper awareness of the changes taking place at Lenox Square.

Double-height handrails make a design statement.

The food court was re-done in a marketplace motif.

Barrel-vaulted ceilings lend light and elegance to the mall's galleries.

Storefronts received top treatment in the renovation of Lenox Square.

An interior view of the renovated Lenox Square.

Renovation or Expansion of an Existing Project

Owner:
JMB Income (Properties LTD XI)
Chicago, Illinois

Architect:
Cooper Carry
Atlanta, Georgia

Designer:
Gar Muse, AIA
Atlanta, Georgia

Certificate of Merit

Riverside Square

Hackensack, New Jersey United States

Gross size of center:
634,687 sq. ft.

Amount of space added or renovated:
81,000 sq. ft.

Gross leasable area excluding anchors:
210,011 sq. ft.

Total acreage of site:
31.5 acres

Type of center:
Fashion/specialty center

Physical description:
Two-level mall

Location of trading area:
Suburban/Urban

Population:
- Primary trading area 356,343
- Secondary trading area 900,000

Development schedule:
- Original opening date March 10, 1977
- Current expansion date November 19, 1995

Parking spaces:
- Present number 3,360

The entrance pylon at Riverside Square.

RIVERSIDE
Square

A planting area.

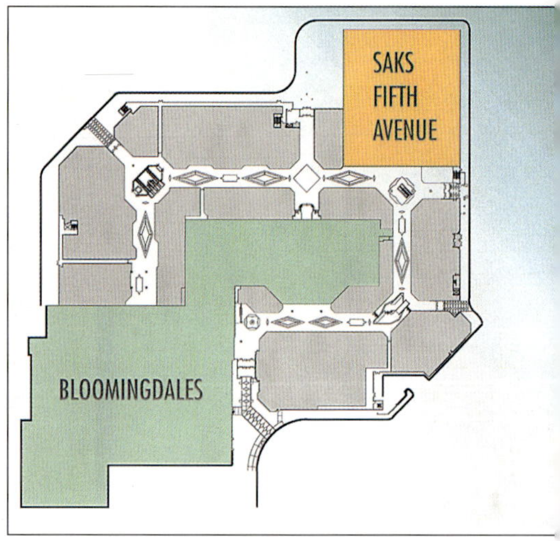

Bloomingdale's and Saks Fifth Avenue clearly identify Riverside Square as a high-end fashion center.

Riverside Square, in the New York City suburb of Hackensack, New Jersey, faced several challenges by the mid-1990s: the expansion and renovation of a competing regional mall; two highways, commercial development, and a wildlife preserve which prevented Riverside Square from expanding its site; and a dark, outdated interior design.

The center decided to undertake extensive renovation and orient itself to an upscale, fashion shopper through a design based in the history of fashion itself. From logo to lighting, every aspect of the new Riverside Square reflects the work of five of the most influential fashion designers in history: Christian Dior, Christobal Balenciaga, Charles Worth, Madeleine Vionnet, and Mariano Fortuny. The renovated mall would be identified with five galleries, each separated by courts or department stores. Each designer's style would influence the furnishing of the seating areas, the lighting design, and the floor patterns.

Linking the five galleries are six courts fashioned with natural marbles from Europe and Mexico. A unique guardrail resembling a needle and thread (post and handrail) follows the center's fashion theme.

MAJOR TENANTS

NAME	TYPE	GLA (SQ. FT.)
Bloomingdale's	Department store	290,346
Saks Fifth Avenue	Department store	107,000
Pottery Barn	Housewares	28,092

Design influences are seen throughout the mall—in a floor medallion, a gallery, and in seating areas.

Physical orientation had been confusing, due to the old mall's figure-8 shape. The angular approach was straightened out in renovation, creating additional leasable area. The earlier low mall ceilings were demolished. New ceilings of Gypsum board were installed, up-lit with continuous cove lighting.

New guardrails, which define the upper-level floor openings, are constructed of tempered glass, bronze, and painted custom metal structural posts and feature decorative metal grill design.

Expiration of leases of existing tenants and the desire to attract the most appropriate tenants created a leasing plan that continued after the renovation was completed.

Safety was of paramount concern during renovation. Temporary ramps, walking surfaces, barricades, and overhead scaffolding were used. A complete logistics manual was prepared by the contractor and architect and incorporated into the bid documents for the subcontractors.

New amenities included a full-service customer assistance desk, luxurious landscaping, fresh flowers, a concierge, valet-attended restrooms, and a children's room. Marketing support involved a new logo and tying in a unified graphics program referencing the architectural motifs. New tenant criteria address the need to replace most tenants with others more in keeping with the specialty center approach.

Transforming Riverside Square from a typical regional mall (in a market already crowded with them) into a high-end fashion center with fashion-influenced design has, the developer says, reversed the mall's recent trend of declining sales and been well received by the community.

Elegant elevator cabs are only one of several attractive new design features in Riverside's renovation.

Design amenities include grillwork on guardrails.

Mall entrance door pulls.

High-end tenants merit high-style storefronts.

A concierge assists shoppers.

Renovation or Expansion of an Existing Project

Owner:
Kimco Realty Corporation
New Hyde Park, New York

Architect:
Arrowstreet, Inc.
Somerville, Massachusetts

Certificate of Merit

Rockingham Mall

Salem, New Hampshire United States

Gross size of center:
330,584 sq. ft.

Amount of space added or renovated:
105,000 sq. ft.

Gross leasable area excluding anchors:
330,584 sq. ft.

Total acreage of site:
38 acres

Type of center:
Power center

Physical description:
Strip

Location of trading area:
Suburban

Population:
- Primary trading area
  144,442
- Secondary trading area
  773,271

Development schedule:
- Original opening date
  June 15, 1975
- Current expansion date
  April 15, 1995
- Future expansion
  September 15, 1997
  20,000 sq. ft. GLA to be added

Parking spaces:
- Present number
  1,550
- 105 parking spaces added

Rockingham Mall's updated look makes a strong statement at one of its entrances.

When it opened as an enclosed mall in 1975, Rockingham Mall was the premier shopping center in Salem, New Hampshire, offering area shoppers the merchandise they wanted from such national chains as Bradlees, Child World, Stop and Shop, and specialty stores. After changes in the economy and the opening of a super-regional mall nearby, Rockingham Mall was 50 percent empty by 1994, with no tenants between its two anchors.

Purchase of Rockingham Mall by its current owner in March 1994 led to a near-complete overhaul of the center's design, tenant mix, and target audience. The enclosed mall was transformed into a strip center of power retailers that also contained a much smaller enclosed mall.

The mall needed to be reconfigured to accommodate three new mini-anchors. The architects demolished 35,000 sq. ft. of mall space and stores but, by eliminating the mall's common area, actually increased the total leasable area by 5,000 sq. ft. Removing the front of the mall also allowed for 120 more parking spaces. There are now 11 small stores and six kiosks, in addition to the six power retailers.

The mall was kept open through careful phased construction and staggered tenant move-in. (One of the existing anchors, T.J. Maxx, insisted on remaining open throughout the renovation, even though it was being relocated. Traffic in the store actually increased during construction, the developer says.)

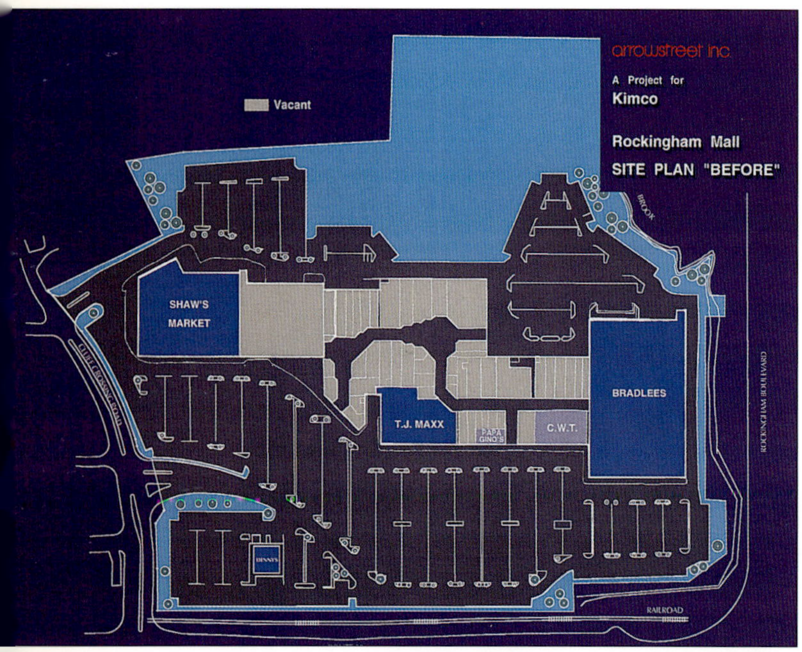

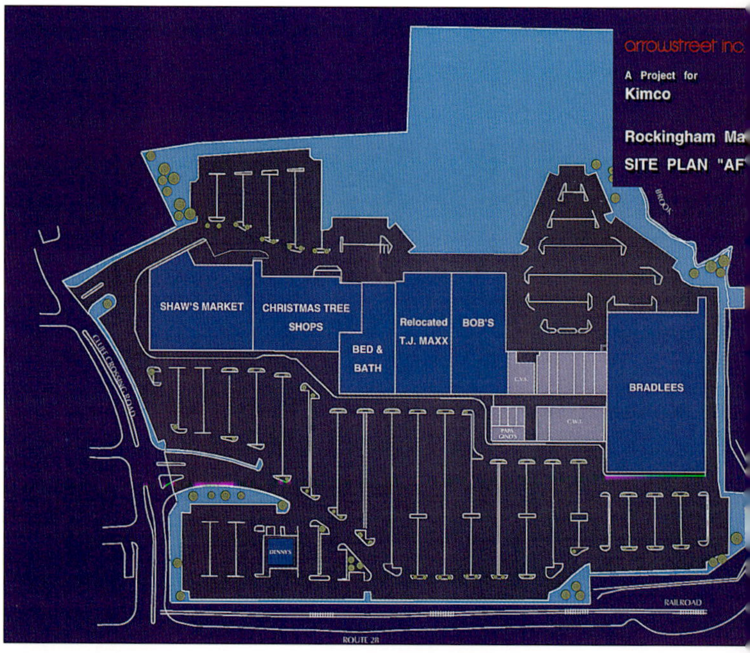

Before-and-after site plans show how the mall area was reconfigured to allow space for power retailer mini-anchors.

MAJOR TENANTS

NAME	TYPE	GLA (SQ. FT.)
Bradlees	Discount department store	90,375
Shaw's Supermarket	Supermarket	51,507
Bob's Stores	Apparel	43,905
Christmas Tree Shops	Holiday decorations	43,875
T.J. Maxx	Apparel	35,000
Bed & Bath	Housewares	24,374

Before-and-after photographs show how a desolate castle became a light, bright shopping destination.

Some small tenants were relocated from areas scheduled for reuse or demolition. Construction of the new exterior wall took place largely in a 15-foot-wide construction "corridor" behind the reconfigured T.J. Maxx space. Use of the largely hidden corridor minimized the construction "look" and the potential hazard to shoppers.

All significant interruptions in services, as well as several key construction processes, occurred either before or after normal operating hours, including the demolition of the abandoned T.J. Maxx store.

Along with the center's reconfiguration, a new value image was created. The exterior was enlivened with new finishes, color, and three-dimensional-design entry pediment features. New plantings, including cherry trees, were added.

From a market perspective, Rockingham Mall now complements the high-end super-regional mall with a value center that is enjoying renewed shopper interest.

The mall area is accessible through several well-designed entrances.

Anchors are an easy walk from smaller retailers.

Design amenities create a new image for power retailing.

Stores get bold signage.

Renovation or Expansion of an Existing Project

Owner:
The RREEF Funds, Inc.
Chicago, Illinois

Architect/Designer:
Architectural Alliance, Inc.
Minneapolis, Minnesota

Certificate of Merit

Woodland Hills Mall

Tulsa, Oklahoma
United States

Gross size of center:
1,005,376 sq. ft.

Amount of space added or renovated:
1,005,376 sq. ft.

Gross leasable area excluding anchors:
383,741 sq. ft.

Total acreage of site:
152 acres

Type of center:
Super-regional center

Physical description:
Enclosed mall

Location of trading area:
Suburban

Population:
- Primary trading area
  670,978

Development schedule:
- Original opening date
  August 4, 1976
- Current renovation date
  January 1996

Parking spaces:
- Present number
  6,200

The new entrance at the renovated Woodland Hills Mall.

WOODLAND HILLS
MALL

Woodland Hills Mall's original design was based on a linear shopping thoroughfare punctuated by retail courts at each of the four department stores and at center court. While designed as a two-level center, its image was that of two single-level malls, one atop the other, with minimal visual interaction between them. Tenants felt the first level was less desirable because of its darkness.

To create a new, fresh image and attract upscale tenants, a renovation would address lighting, ceiling and flooring, columns, furniture, graphics, and other design issues.

A key objective was to increase both natural and artificial lighting levels. Light coves and new ceiling soffits were added. Large-scale custom-designed light fixtures such as chandeliers and wall sconces complement new energy-efficient ambient lighting. Eighteen new glass skylights were installed, including two rotundas in center court.

With graceful bird sculptures overhead, major courts feature a new carousel and a fountain.

MAJOR TENANTS		
NAME	**TYPE**	**GLA (SQ. FT.)**
Dillard's	Department store	179,128
Foley's	Department store	160,003
Sears	Department store	156,166
JC Penney	Department store	126,333

Kiosks located in the improved mall environment.

The arch of outside pylons and mall entrances is repeated in floor tile patterns.

The site plan shows an angled mall area, making improved sightlines between floors especially important.

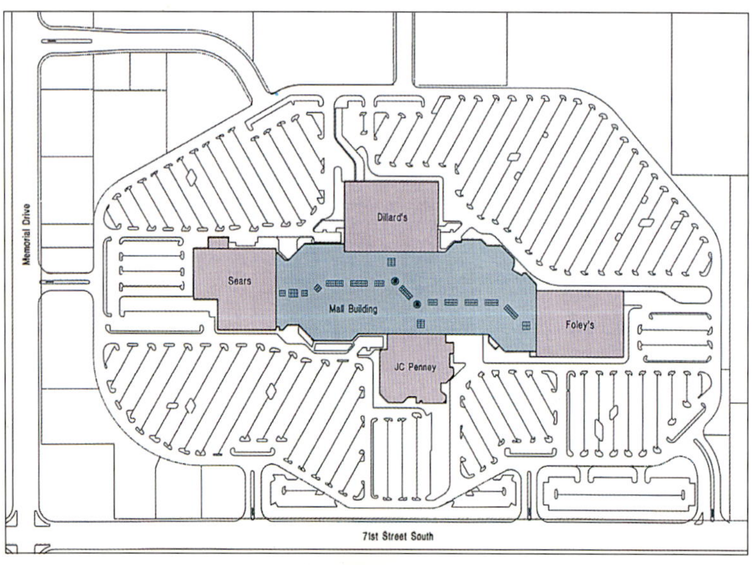

Sightlines between the first and second floors were improved. To flood the first floor with natural light, second-floor openings were greatly enlarged. New glass guardrails improved sightlines as well.

Existing built-in seating was replaced with a flexible furniture system. New graphics, a fresh color scheme, and stone tile floors revitalized the common area. Restrooms were improved, including the addition of restrooms for families and for assisted-care customers.

Woodland Hills' exterior benefited from new pylons at site entrances and illuminated directional signage. Glass-arched mall entries were installed.

Woodland Hills Mall's pylon gives the center a much more striking presence than it had in earlier days (below).

Marketing support communicated to shoppers that there would be minimal inconvenience during construction, since all work would be done at night. A character named Fred would help deliver renovation-focused messages. Fred was a construction worker who left home and family each night to work on Woodland Hills Mall's Classic Renovation. Fred appeared in TV and radio commercials and on in-mall directories, delivering his message that "Fred's working nights so that you can shop days at Woodland Hills Mall." The real construction workers took to Fred, posting his picture over their time clock with the question: "Has anyone seen this man?"

Renovation helped the mall secure many upscale merchants, including Abercrombie & Fitch, The Body Shop, Godiva Chocolatier, and Talbots. JC Penney and Sears also chose to remodel their stores in 1996, and Dillard's plans a renovation and expansion in 1997. The developer feels that the Woodland Hills Mall renovation "is a perfect example of a pro-active strategy of not waiting until the competition makes its move."

Glass guardrails and brighter ceilings contribute to the fresh look at Woodland Hills.